Tipbook
Acoustic Guitar

This publication is not authorised for sale in the United States of America and/or Canada.

Exclusive Distributor for the UK:

Music Sales Limited, Distribution Centre, Newmarket Road,
Bury St Edmunds, Suffolk IP33 3YB, UK.

Typeset in Glasgow and Minion.

Printed in The Netherlands.

No part of this book may be reproduced in any form without prior written permission from the publisher except for the quotation of brief passages in reviews.

The publisher and author have done their best to ensure the accuracy and currency of all the information in the Tipbook, however, they can accept no responsibility for any loss, injury or inconvenience sustained as a result of information or advice contained in the guide. Trademarks, user names, and certain illustrations have been used in this book solely to identify the products or instruments discussed. Such use does not identify endorsement by or affiliation with the trademark owner(s).

© 2007 THE TIPBOOK COMPANY BV, The Netherlands

ISBN 978-1-84772-072-6

Order No. AM990473

www.musicsales.com

Hugo Pinksterboer

Tipbook
Acoustic Guitar

Handy, clearly written, and up-to-date.
The reference manual for both beginners and
advanced guitar players, including Tipcodes and a
glossary.

Wise Publications
part of The Music Sales Group

London • New York • Paris • Sydney • Copenhagen • Berlin • Madrid • Tokyo

Thanks
For their information, their expertise, their time, and their help we'd like to thank the following musicians, teachers, technicians and other guitar experts: Harry Sacksioni, Erik Vaarzon Morel, Olaf Tarenskeen, the late Willy Heijnen (*Meet Music Magazine*), Ulbo de Sitter, Arno van den Wijngaard (Feedback), Harm van der Geest, Frans van Ingen (*Music Maker*), Corrie de Haan, Nicky Moeken (*Gitaar Plus*), Ron Houben (Houben Guitars), Chris Teerlink and Martin van der Lucht (Luthiers Gutars), Gilbert Maurice Herngreen, Harry de Jonge (Sacksioni Guitars), Henny van Ochten (Texas & Tweed), Nils Rurack and Michel de Groot.

We also wish to thank Teja Gerken (*Acoustic Guitar magazine*) for his last-minute assistance, Elliot Freedman for his valuable input, Nahim Avci (Rotterdam Conservatory) Roy op de Kamp (Papen & Bongaerts), Harold Koenders (JIC), Ivar Lelieveld (Muziekhandel Dijkman), Ben van der Sman (Casa Benelly), Niek Stoop, Rick Verhoeff (BMI), and Bart Witte (Dirk Witte Muziek) for their help, guitarist and writer John van der Veer for being a valuable and ever-present source of information, editor and guitarist Michiel Roelse (*Gitarist*) for his contribution to the book, and Gerard Braun for his musical help in making the Tipcode-movies.

Anything missing?
Any omissions? Any areas that could be improved? Please go to www.tipbook.com to contact us; thanks!

Acknowledgements
Concept, design, and illustrations: Gijs Bierenbroodspot
Cover photo: René Vervloet
Translation: MdJ Copy & Translation
Editor: Robert L. Doerschuk
Proofreaders: Nancy Bishop and René de Graaff

IN BRIEF

Have you just started playing? Are you thinking about buying an acoustic guitar? Or do you want to find out more about the instrument you already own? This book will tell you everything you need to know. There's an introduction to the instrument and to lessons and practicing, and there's information about buying, selecting, and play-testing guitars, about strings, picks, and nails, about acoustic/ electric and bass guitars, about tuning and maintenance, about the guitar's history and family members, and much more.

The best you can
After reading this Tipbook, you'll be able to get the most out of your guitar, to buy the best instrument possible, and to easily understand any other literature on the subject, from magazines to books and Internet publications.

Begin at the beginning
If you have just started playing, or haven't yet begun, pay particular attention to the first four chapters. If you have been playing longer, you may prefer to skip ahead to Chapter 5. Please note that all prices mentioned in this book reflect only approximate street prices in US dollars.

Glossary
The glossary at the end of the book briefly explains most of the terms you'll come across as a guitar player. To make life even easier, it doubles as an index.

Hugo Pinksterboer

TIPBOOK ACOUSTIC GUITAR

CONTENTS

VIII SEE WHAT YOU READ WITH TIPCODE
www.tipbook.com
The Tipcodes in this book give you access to additional information (short movies, soundtracks, photos, etc.) at www.tipbook.com. Here's how it works.

1 CHAPTER 1. A GUITARIST?
Guitarists play in concert halls, around campfires, and in nightclubs and stadiums, playing rock, classical music, children's songs or anything else.

5 CHAPTER 2. A QUICK TOUR
From body and neck to frets and braces: the instrument in bird's-eye view, and the differences between classical and steel-string guitars.

15 CHAPTER 3. LEARNING TO PLAY
How easy is it to learn to play guitar? Will you need to take lessons? You'll find the answers in this chapter, which also deals with practicing and reading music.

22 CHAPTER 4. BUYING A GUITAR
A guide to prices, buying new or secondhand, and other tips before you go out to buy a guitar.

26 CHAPTER 5. A GOOD GUITAR
Tips for comparing and play-testing guitars, so that you choose the best possible instrument.

49 CHAPTER 6. ACOUSTIC/ELECTRIC GUITARS
Everything you need to know about acoustic guitars with built-in pickups.

55 CHAPTER 7. STRINGS
Good strings allow you to get the best out of your guitar. A chapter on the various materials, gauges, windings and tensions.

62 CHAPTER 8. CLEANING AND CHANGING STRINGS
Strings sound best when they're kept clean and put on properly.

74 CHAPTER 9. TUNING
Various ways to tune guitars. Includes tips on tuning forks, electronic tuners and open tunings.

84 CHAPTER 10. PICKS AND NAILS
Tips for good picks and strong nails.

88 CHAPTER 11. MAINTENANCE AND CLEANING
A clean guitar looks better, plays better, and sells better. Includes tips for on the road.

94 CHAPTER 12. BACK IN TIME
A lot of history in very few words.

97 CHAPTER 13. THE FAMILY
Meet some of the guitar's closest family members.

105 CHAPTER 14. HOW THEY'RE MADE
Guitars are made in huge factories as well as in small workshops. A guided tour.

108 CHAPTER 15. BRANDS
The main guitar brands lined up.

112 GLOSSARY AND INDEX
What is a solid top, a piezo pickup, or a compensated saddle? A guitar player's glossary. It doubles as an index, so you can use it as a handy reference.

121 TIPCODE LIST
All acoustic guitar Tipcodes listed.

122 WANT TO KNOW MORE?
Information about other resources, and about the makers of the Tipbook Series.

125 ESSENTIAL DATA
Two pages for essential notes on your equipment.

TIPBOOK ACOUSTIC GUITAR

SEE WHAT YOU READ WITH TIPCODE

www.tipbook.com

In addition to the many illustrations on the following pages, Tipbooks offer you an additional way to see – and even hear – what you are reading about. The *Tipcodes* that you will come across regularly in this book give you access to extra pictures, short movies, soundtracks, and other additional information at www.tipbook.com.

Here is how it works: On page 29 of this book there's a paragraph on *fingerpicking*. Right above that paragraph it says **Tipcode AGTR-005**. Type in that code on the Tipcode page at www.tipbook.com and you will see a short movie that shows this technique. Similar movies are available on a variety of subjects.

Enter code, watch movie
You enter the Tipcode beneath the movie window on the Tipcode page. In most cases, you will then see the relevant images within five to ten seconds. Tipcodes activate a short movie, sound, or both, or a series of photos.

Tipcodes listed
You can find all the Tipcodes used in this book in a single list on page 121.

Quick start
The movies, photo series and soundtracks are designed so that they start quickly. If you miss something the first time, you can of course repeat them. And if it all happens too fast, use the pause button beneath the movie window.

TIPCODE

First, make your selection: Tipcode, chords and fingering charts, or the glossary.

The Tipcode window displays movies, photo series, fingering charts, chords, and explanations of the words used in this book.

Enter a Tipcode here and click on the button. Want to see it again? Click again.

These links take you directly to other interesting sites.

Plug-ins

If the software you need to view the movies or photos is not yet installed on your computer, you'll automatically be told which software you need, and where you can sdownload it. This kind of software (*plug-ins*) is free.

Still more at www.tipbook.com

You can find even more information at www.tipbook.com. For instance, you can look up words in the glossaries of all the Tipbooks published to date. For clarinetists, saxophonists and flutists there are fingering charts, for drummers there are the rudiments, and for guitarists and pianists there are chord diagrams. Also included are links to some of the websites mentioned in the *Want to Know More?* section of each Tipbook.

1. A GUITARIST?

Guitarists can play a few chords to accompany a song, or a virtuoso solo over the solid foundation of a four-piece rock band. They can also play a classical concert, alone or with a full-sized orchestra, or accompany a dance group, or a choir. From campfire to stadium concert, from nightclub to living room, acoustic guitarists can play anywhere – and there are almost as many different guitars as there are guitarists.

Because they can play several notes simultaneously (*chords*), guitarists can easily make music alone, without a band. In that sense, guitars resemble pianos, home keyboards, or organs, which also allow you to play chords.

Acoustic instruments

Another similarity between acoustic guitars and pianos is that they are both *acoustic* instruments, meaning you can play them without an amplifier. The body acts as a soundbox, acoustically 'amplifying' what you're doing.

And you're the singer

Acoustic guitars are often used mainly for playing chords, and just a couple of different chords are all you need to play a whole bunch of songs. To accompany a singer, for example – who could very well be you. After all, there are lots of singer/guitarists who play entire concerts on their own.

Classical guitarists   Tipcode AGTR-001

Classical guitarists have their own special instruments and techniques. Instead of strumming all the strings at once, as you do when playing chords, they pluck the strings with their fingers and nails. What's more, classical guitarists always play sitting down, usually with the instrument resting on their left thigh, using a small footrest for their left foot. Other guitarists usually support the guitar's body with their right thigh when playing seated.

Different strokes
Plucking the strings with your fingers sounds completely different from strumming them with a *pick*. Another difference? *Slide guitarists* slide along the strings with a tube, instead of stopping them with their fingertips. And even when two guitarists play the same acoustic guitar the same way, you'll hear two different sounds…

Popular instrument
The acoustic guitar is one of the world's most popular instruments. Here's why.
- They're very affordable. **It won't cost you much money** to buy yourself a guitar you can enjoy for years to come – although you can just as easily spend a couple of months' wages on one.
- The guitar is **not difficult** to learn. That doesn't mean you'll soon be finished learning either; in the end, the guitar is as hard to master as the piano, the drums, or the saxophone. Or just as easy.
- A guitar **weighs next to nothing**, so you can easily take it along wherever you go.
- Acoustic guitars aren't loud enough to annoy your neighbors, but there's **no need for an amplifier** to hear what you're doing.

The two main kinds
The two most common acoustic guitars are the *steel-string guitar* and the *classical guitar*. Each is known by a number of other names as well.

Classical, Spanish, or nylon-string
The classical guitar is mainly used for classical guitar music, of course. It is also known as the *Spanish guitar*, as that was the country where it was given its final form. A third name, to distinguish it from steel-string instruments, is *nylon-string guitar*.

Classical, Spanish or nylon-string guitar.

Steel-string guitar, western guitar, folk guitar

Steel-string guitars originally come from the US. The names *western guitar* and *folk guitar* are also often used. Steel-string guitars sound louder and brighter than classical guitars.

Steel-string, western, or folk guitar.

Even more

There are many more types of acoustic guitars – twelve-string guitars, for example, or resonator guitars, which have metal bodies, acoustic bass guitars with four or five strings, and acoustic/electric guitars, which you can hook up to an amplifier, just like an electric guitar.

Their own sound

All these different guitars have a sound or *timbre* of their own. A sound that suits a certain style of music, like the flamenco guitar or the jazz guitar. Or a certain way of playing, like the twelve-string guitar; its pleasant, broad sound is perfect for playing chords.

Acoustic or electric

Many guitarists play both acoustic and electric instruments, usually starting out on an acoustic one and switching to an electric guitar after a couple of years – but plenty of electric players decide to add an acoustic instrument later in their careers too.

An electric/acoustic guitar can be hooked up to an amplifier. The controls of the guitar are usually located on the upper bout.

2. A QUICK TOUR

Seen from a distance, a guitar seems to be nothing more than a body in the shape of a huge figure-8, and a neck. When you get closer, there's a lot more to see. An introduction to the main parts of the instrument, starting with the classical guitar, then the steel-string guitar and finally the acoustic/electric guitar.

One look at the *head* will usually tell you whether you're dealing with a classical or a steel-string guitar. If it is slotted, you're probably looking at a classical, nylon-string guitar. Most steel-string instruments have a solid head. Heads are also referred to as *headstocks* or *pegheads*.

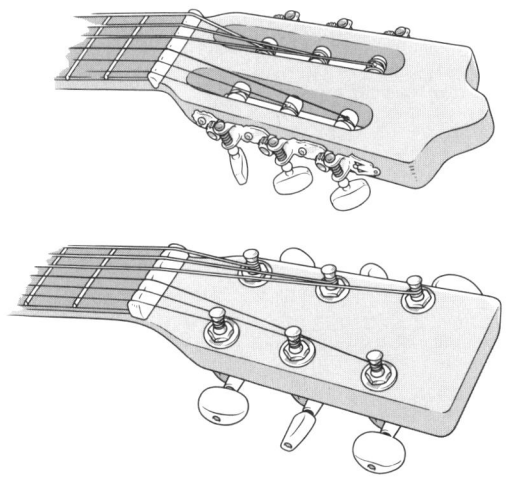

The slotted head of a classical guitar, and the solid head of a steel-string guitar.

CHAPTER 2

THE CLASSICAL GUITAR.

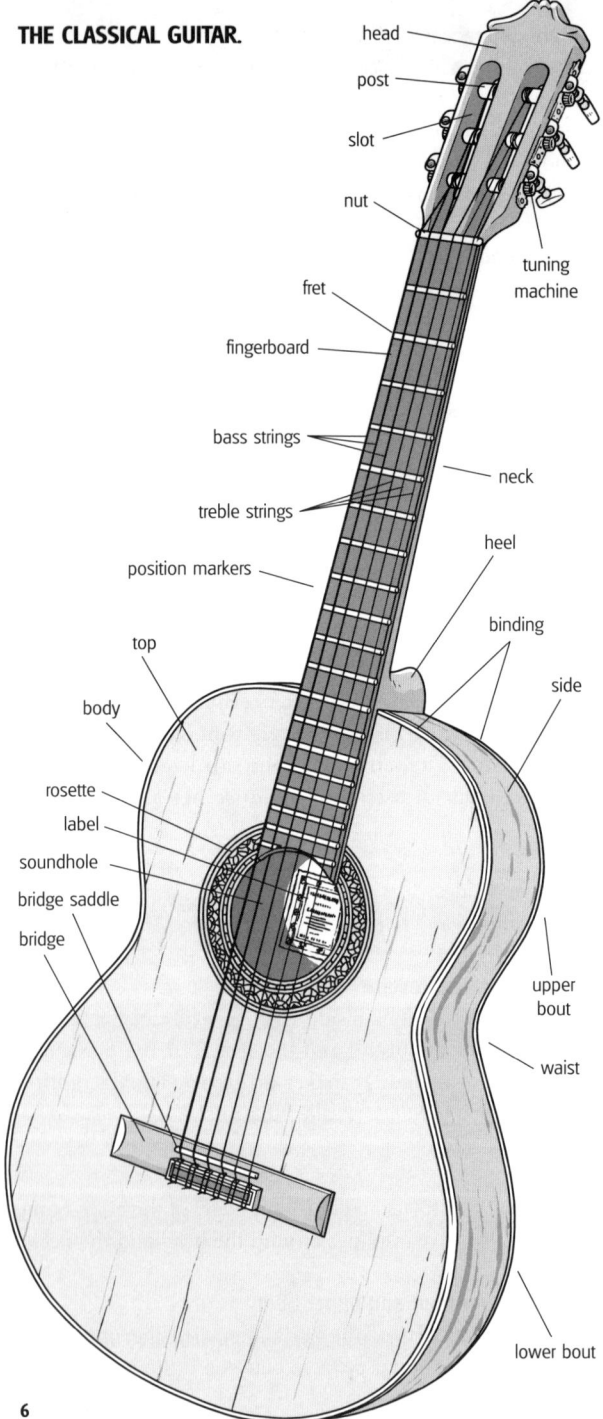

More differences
Three more differences: Steel-string models usually have larger bodies and narrower necks, they often have a *pickguard* to protect the body against scratches by picks and nails, and you can clearly see that the three thinnest strings are made of steel, rather than of nylon.

The sound   Tipcode AGTR-002
Classical guitars also have a different sound, mainly because of the strings. They sound warmer, mellower or 'drier' than steel-string guitars, which sound brighter and – of course – more metallic. The sound of steel strings also projects better.

CLASSICAL GUITARS
If you look only at all the main parts and what they do, a classical guitar is not that much different from a steel-string instrument.

The top
The wood of the body's *top* is very important for the sound of the instrument, as you can tell from its second name – *soundboard*. The left side of the top is often the exact mirror image of the right side; if so, it's a *bookmatched* top.

Back and sides
Between top and *back* are the *sides* or *rims*.

Soundhole and rosette
When you take a look inside, there's usually a label bearing the name of the brand and the series, or the name and signature of the guitar maker or *luthier*. The decoration around the *soundhole* is called the *rosette*.

Binding
The *bindings* protect and finish the edges of the body. Some guitars also have bindings around the head and the neck.

Waist, lower bout and upper bout
The broader parts of the body are called the *upper bout* and the *lower bout* or *belly*. In between is the *waist*.

Heel
The *heel* is the wooden block at the point where the neck is attached to the body.

Fingerboard
The strings run along the *fingerboard*, onto which you press your fingers to *stop* the strings. Stopping a string shortens the section of the string that vibrates, thus producing a higher pitch.

Frets
The small metal strips on the fingerboard are the *frets*. They make a guitar easier to play in tune than a violin or a cello, for example, which have no frets.

Fretboard
Because of the frets, the fingerboard is also known as *fretboard*. 'Playing the fourth fret' means pressing the string just behind the fourth fret. Stopping a string is also known as *fretting* a string.

Position markers
On the side of the fingerboard that you face while playing, you may find a series of *position markers* or *markers* – small dots that indicate the fret or the *position* you're at.

Posts and tuners
The strings are wound around the *string posts*. You tune the guitar with the *tuning machines* or *tuners*, either tightening or loosening the strings.

Strings
The thinnest, highest-sounding string is called the *first string*. The thickest string, or the *sixth string*, sounds the lowest. As a reminder: The thinnest string has the 'thinnest' number, 1. The thickest string has a thick-looking number, the 6.

E, A, D, G, B, E
The six strings, from thick to thin, low to high, are tuned to the notes E, A, D, G, B, E. These pitches can be easily memorized as Eating And Drinking Give Brain Energy; two more memory aids can be found in Chapter 9.

Wound strings
You can easily see that the thin strings are made of nylon. The three thickest ones are nylon too, but they look quite different because they're wound with metal wire. Their name is obvious: *wound* strings.

Bass and treble
Wound strings are also known as *bass strings*. The *plain strings* are also known as *treble strings*, or *melody strings*.

Nut
After they leave the tuning machines, the strings cross the *nut*. This thin strip makes sure that the strings run at the right height over the neck. The grooves in the nut make sure they do so at equal distances from each other.

Bridge and saddle
At the other end, the strings tie around the *bridge*. The light-colored strip on the bridge that supports the strings is called the *bridge saddle*.

Confusing
Some guitarists use 'bridge' to refer to either the saddle or the nut. Pretty confusing, unless you know this in advance.

STEEL-STRING GUITARS
Steel-string guitars come in many different sizes and shapes, of which the Jumbo and the Dreadnought are the two biggest. Chapters 5 and 13 tell you more about those sizes. The names of the main parts of the guitar, from body to headstock, have been mentioned above.

Pickguard
The pickguard protects the top from nails and picks, that may otherwise scratch it when strumming chords – which is what steel-string guitars are often used for.

The fourteenth fret
The body usually starts at the fourteenth fret instead of the twelfth, as on classical guitars. To use the lingo: most steel-string guitars have a *fourteen-fret neck*.

CHAPTER 2

THE STEEL-STRING GUITAR.

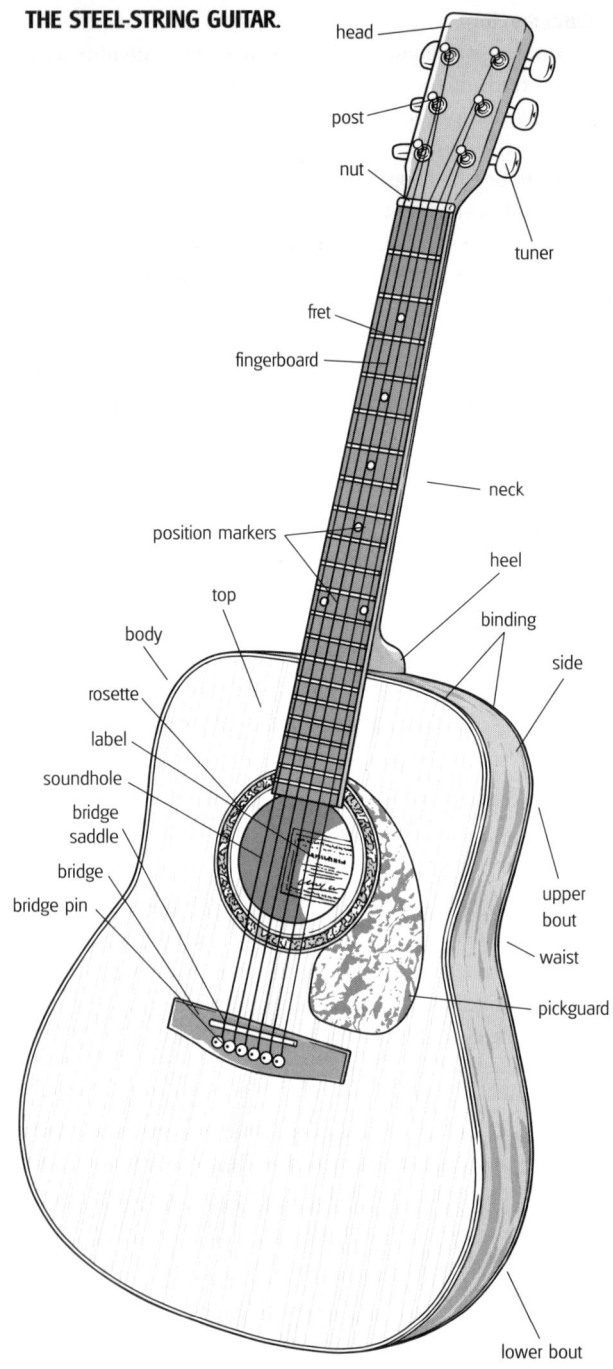

Cutaway
Some steel-string guitars also have a *cutaway*, giving easier access to the highest positions on the neck. You'll find two examples on pages 30–31.

Markers and bindings
Steel-string guitars have *position markers* on the side of the neck and on the fingerboard. The bindings often have special patterns, such as the popular herringbone.

Plain and wound strings
Most steel-string guitars have two thin *plain strings* and four thicker *wound strings*. Their standard tuning is identical to that of a nylon-string guitar: E, A, D, G, B, E (from thick to thin, from low to high).

A narrower neck
The neck of a steel-string guitar is narrower than that of a classical guitar. If you look along the neck from the headstock you'll see it is slightly curved – a bit higher underneath the middle strings, with a very slight downward slope toward the outer strings.

Truss rod
Steel strings pull harder than nylon strings. To counteract that extra tension, an adjustable metal *truss rod* is built into the neck.

Bridge
The bridges on most steel-string guitars have a distinctive shape, which often allows you to tell the make of the instrument.

Bridge saddle
The bridge saddle is usually not at a right angle to the strings, and sometimes consists of two or more parts. Both of these design features are ways to get the instrument to play in tune.

Bridge pins
Right behind the bridge saddle you can see the heads of the *bridge pins* which hold the strings in place. Bridge pins are also known as *pegs*.

CHAPTER 2

Flattops and archtops

The name *flattop* distinguishes steel-string guitars with a flat top from instruments with an arched top. *Arch-top guitars* are somewhat similar to violins in appearance, both because of their shape and because they often have two *f*-shaped soundholes.

An arch-top guitar with *f*-shaped soundholes.

THE INSIDE

Classical and steel-string guitars differ on the inside as well. As a player this won't concern you too much, but you can't open a guitar magazine or book without reading about *braces* – so here they are.

Bracing

The top is strengthened on the inside by a number of braces, which also influence the sound. Most classical guitars have *fan-bracing*, seven braces, laid out in the shape of a fan. The braces against the back are called *ribs* or *struts*.

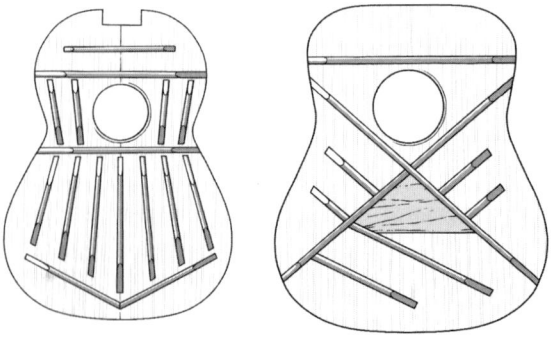

Left: the braces of a classical guitar (fan-bracing); right: the braces of a steel-string guitar (X-bracing).

Pattern
The braces in steel-string guitars have a different pattern. The so-called *X-bracing* is the traditional and most common type.

LEFT-HANDED
Most left-handed guitarists play 'right-handed' guitars. After all, their quicker left hand often plays at least as big a role as their right hand. Others prefer a left-handed guitar, strumming or plucking the strings with their left hand and stopping them with their right. A classical guitar can be adapted for left-handed players quite easily, although it takes more than just putting the strings on the other way around.

A steel-string guitar for left-handed guitarists.

Adapting guitars
Adapting a steel-string guitar is a bit harder, if only because the pattern of the braces underneath the thick strings differs from that underneath the thin ones. If you reversed the strings, you'd have to reverse the bracing as well, which is too much work. However, cheaper steel-string guitars are sometimes converted for left-handed use without adapting the braces, with no major consequences for the sound.

Better solution
A better solution is to buy a guitar that has been built to be used left-handed. There are fewer such guitars to choose from, and you often pay just a bit extra, though for more expensive guitars the difference in price may be as much as a hundred dollars or more. If you prefer a guitar with

a cutaway, you'll just have to get a left-handed model. Otherwise, the cutaway will be on the upper shoulder of the guitar, where it is no use at all.

ACOUSTIC/ELECTRIC GUITARS

If your guitar isn't loud enough, you can stick a microphone in front of it. Most guitarists, however, prefer a guitar with a built-in pickup. That way they can hook it up directly to an amplifier, just like an electric guitar. Acoustic guitars with built-in pickups are known as *acoustic/electric* (*A/E*) or *electro-acoustic guitars*. Usually these are 'regular' steel-string guitars, the only difference being the pickup and the electronics that come with it.

Pickup

A pickup literally 'picks up' the vibrations of the strings, translating them into electric signals which can be amplified. Most acoustic/electric guitars have *piezo pickups*, invisibly mounted under the saddle of the guitar. Chapter 6, *Acoustic/electric guitars*, tells you all about them.

Controls

Controls for volume, tone, and other parameters are usually located on the upper bout of the guitar, invisible to the audience. They operate the built-in *preamplifier* or *preamp*, which boosts the signal before sending it out to the main amp.

The control panel of an acoustic/electric guitar.

TIPBOOK ACOUSTIC GUITAR

3. LEARNING TO PLAY

Is it hard to play the guitar? That depends on what you want. You can learn the chords to a couple of songs in a few weeks. But what if you want to play classical music, or if you want to master more than a couple of chords? A chapter on chord charts, lessons, notes, and practicing – and on how easy it can be.

If you want to play classical guitar music, you can't get around learning to read notes. Yet many guitarists in other styles don't use traditional notation. They rely on chord charts or tablature, which are two different ways to put guitar music on paper.

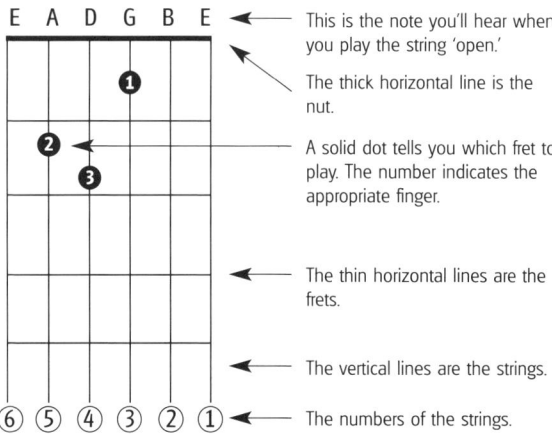

This is the note you'll hear when you play the string 'open.'

The thick horizontal line is the nut.

A solid dot tells you which fret to play. The number indicates the appropriate finger.

The thin horizontal lines are the frets.

The vertical lines are the strings.

The numbers of the strings.

Play string 3 at the first fret with your index finger, play string 5 at the second fret with your middle finger, and play string 4 at the second fret with your ring finger. The result is an E-major chord.

CHAPTER 3

Three or four chords
Many famous songs in many popular styles of music consist of only three or four chords – from the blues and the Beatles to Metallica and Madonna. Once you learn those chords by heart and practice them for a couple of weeks, you'll be able to play plenty of tunes.

Chord charts   Tipcode AGTR-003
If you want to learn chords, all you need is a book containing *chord charts* – diagrams that simply indicate where to put your fingers for each different chord.

The blues
Here's an example of what you can do with chord charts: Just learn the three chords below, and you can play a twelve-bar blues tune.

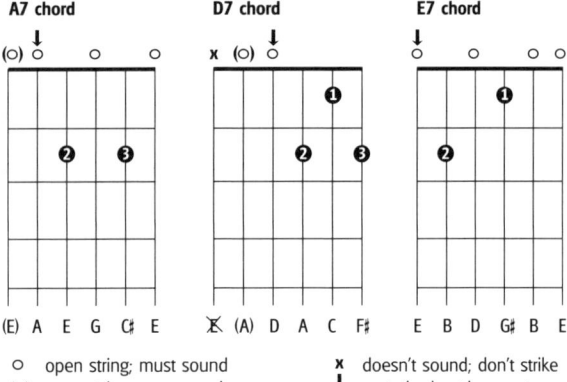

To play a twelve-bar blues tune, all you need are these three simple chords. Each of the twelve bars consists of four beats. Play 1x (one bar, equaling four counts) A7, 1xD7, 2xA7, 2xD7, 2xA7, 1xE7, 1xD7, 1xA7 and 1xE7. Repeat this as long as you like. The last time around, you replace the E7 in the last bar by A7.

Tablature
Another way to put music on paper without notes is the *tablature* or *tab system*. This is often used to notate guitar solos and bass lines in the songbooks that are available in most music stores. Usually the 'regular' notes are included to indicate the precise rhythm, because tablature doesn't allow for that. Exercise books in tablature are also available.

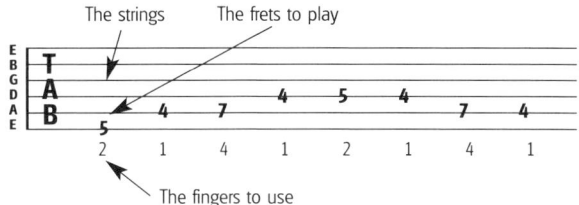

The tablature staff represents a guitar neck.

Reading music

With the exception of classical players, there are thousands of guitarists who don't read music – including some who are quite famous. However, it may not be a bad idea to learn the traditional notation too, even if classical music is not your thing. Here are some reasons why.

- You'll have access to **loads of books and magazines** with exercises, songs, and solos – even when they're not in tablature.
- It'll give you **a better insight** into the way chords and songs are structured.
- It enables you to **put down on paper** your own songs, solos, ideas, and exercises.
- The ability to read music makes you **more of a musician**, instead of 'just' a guitarist.
- And finally: Learning to read music **isn't that hard at all**. *Tipbook Music on Paper – Basic Theory* teaches you the basics within a few chapters.

LESSONS

Hardly anybody learns to play classical guitar music without taking lessons, as it's very hard to master classical guitar technique on your own. For other types of music, consulting a teacher isn't a bad idea either.

Not classical

Of course you can work out everything on your own, but why would you when there are people who can teach you. Or they can at least tell you the basics, so that you start out the right way. Again, there are plenty of famous guitarists who wouldn't know what a music teacher looked like. There are also plenty of famous guitarists who have had lessons. And quite a few of them still do, occasionally.

Learning more

Good teachers not only teach good technique, they will work on a good tone and good posture too, and on reading music, tuning, and playing different styles of music. You name it. Fact is, classical lessons are a good start, even if you think you're going to end up playing something completely different.

Questions, questions

On your first visit to a teacher, don't just ask how much it costs. Here are some other questions.

- Is an **introductory lesson** included? This is a good way to find out how well you get on with the teacher, and for that matter, with the instrument.
- Is the teacher interested in taking you on as a student even if you are doing it **just for the fun of it**, or will he or she expect you to practice at least three hours a day?
- Will you have to make a large investment in method books right away, or is the **course material provided**?
- Can you **record your lessons**, so that you can listen again to how you sounded and what was said when you get home?
- Will you be allowed to concentrate fully on **the style of music you want to play**, or will you be required to learn other styles? Will you be stimulated to do so?
- Will this teacher make you **practice scales** for two years, or will you be encouraged to perform as soon as possible?

Finding a teacher

Looking for a private teacher? Music stores may have teachers on their staff, or be able to refer you to one. You can also consult your local Musician's Union, or the band director at a high school in your area. You can also check the classified ads in newspapers, in music magazines or on supermarket bulletin boards, or consult the *Yellow Pages*. Professional private teachers will usually charge between twenty and fifty dollars per hour. Some make house calls, for which you'll have to pay a little extra.

Group or individual lessons

While most guitar students take individual lessons, you can also try group lessons if that's an option in your area.

Private lessons are more expensive, but can be tailored exactly to your needs.

Collectives
You also may want to check whether there are any teacher collectives or music schools in your area. These collectives may offer extras such as ensemble playing, master classes, and clinics, in a wide variety of styles and at various levels.

PRACTICING
You can learn to play without reading notes. Without a teacher, too. But no one ever learned to play without practicing.

How long?
How long you need to practice depends on what you want to achieve. Many top musicians practiced four to eight hours a day for several years, or more. The more time you spend on it, the faster you improve. But half an hour a day usually results in steady progress.

Hang in there
To start with, playing the guitar will take some getting used to. Especially your left hand, because it gets to do a lot of work, in a rather awkward position. On a steel-string guitar you'll also feel the strings cutting into your fingertips. Hang in there, this will pass.

Acoustic, electric?
Playing an acoustic guitar is different from playing an electric one. It's harder to press down the strings, for one. It also takes more effort to make an acoustic guitar sound really good. This is precisely why the acoustic guitar is an excellent instrument to start on, whether you plan to keep playing acoustic or not. Playing electric will only be made easier.

Books, videos, CDs, and CD-ROMs
Guitarists have easy access to tons of practice and reading material, and there are also tutorial videos and CD-ROMs with guitar lessons.
- **Guitar books** come in all shapes and sizes, for absolute

CHAPTER 3

beginners and absolute pros. Quite a few of them come with tapes or CDs that include examples or play-along exercises; you turn off the sound of the guitarist and play that part yourself.
- Most **guitar and music magazines** offer chord charts, tablature, and other practice materials too.
- **Guitar videos** are usually made by well-known guitarists who show you the tricks of the trade. These video lessons usually last anywhere from thirty to ninety minutes. A booklet with printouts of the recorded rhythms and exercises is sometimes included.
- There are **CD-ROMs** that turn your computer into a guitar teacher – and the Internet offers guitar lessons as well.

Keeping time

You are usually supposed to end a piece in the tempo you started at. So it's good to practice with a metronome, at least once in a while; this is a small device that ticks or beeps out a steady, adjustable pulse, which helps you to work on your tempo, timing, and rhythm.

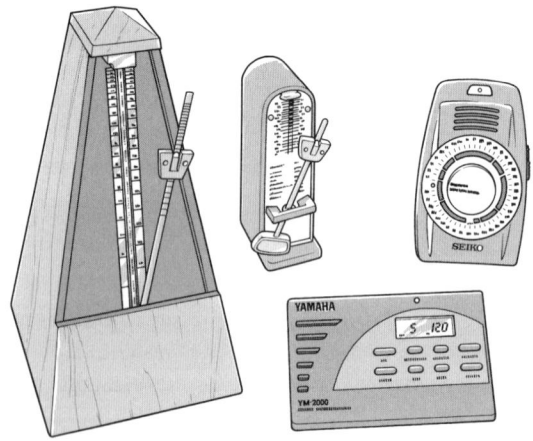

Two mechanical metronomes and two electronic ones.

Electronics and computers

A drum machine is a great alternative to the metronome. There are similar machines that can play bass lines and other programmable instruments too, and there are machines and software programs that offer you an entire band to play along to. Phrase trainers are devices that can slow down a musical phrase from a CD, for example, so you can figure out even the meanest, fastest licks at your own tempo. There is software available that does the same thing.

Record yourself
It's hard to really listen to yourself while you're playing. That's why many musicians record their practice sessions. A Walkman with a built-in microphone is basically all you need, but you'll get more enjoyable and instructive recordings if you use better equipment, such as an minidisc recorder with a separate microphone, or any other more or less professional type of home-recording equipment.

Get to work
And finally; visit festivals, concerts, and sessions. Listen to bands and soloists. One of the best ways to learn to play is through seeing other musicians at work. Living legends or local amateurs – every gig's a learning experience. And the very best way to learn to play? Play a lot!

4. BUYING A GUITAR

One of the nice things about guitars is that you can buy a pretty good instrument for very little money – on the other hand, you can just as easily spend half a year's wages on one. The following chapter tells you everything you'll want to know before going out to buy an instrument. Chapters 5 and 6 deal with what to listen and watch out for once you're in the store.

One to two hundred dollars is all you need to buy a brand new acoustic guitar. This is very little, when you consider that the guitar has to be made, shipped, and sold for that price. So don't expect too much – but you will at least be able to play. A top-of-the-line instrument can easily cost fifty times as much.

Solid top

Most teachers will advise you not to begin on the cheapest guitar you can buy; it's better to spend a little more on a decent instrument, preferably with a solid top (see page 31). These usually start at around two to three hundred dollars.

Great bargains

When buying an acoustic guitar you may come across great bargains: Guitars sometimes sound as if they're worth at least twice or three times their actual price. It may take someone with experience to recognize an instrument like that. So when you go out to buy your first instrument, take a guitarist along – a good one, preferably, who can also tell the poorer-quality guitars that cost just as much, or more…

Why an expensive one?

Spotting the difference between low-budget and expensive guitars isn't that easy, especially since the quality of lower-priced instruments has improved. What exactly are you paying for when you spend more money on a guitar? Better wood, for one thing, and a better sound. Also, more expensive guitars often have higher-quality finish and parts, such as the tuning machines. Or the rosette may have an intricate, finely-detailed inlay, and the markers of a steel-string guitar may be beautifully worked-out designs, instead of your basic dots – things that do nothing for the sound but add a lot to the instrument's exclusivity, or its beauty, and to its price, of course.

The intricately inlaid rosette of a classical guitar.

Handmade

Even two or three hundred dollar guitars are often advertised as 'handmade'. Are they, really? That depends on what you take handmade to mean. Many low-budget Spanish guitars, for example, are indeed built by hand, be it in large factories with assembly lines. However, when they talk about 'real' handmade guitars, players are referring to master *luthiers* who build a guitar from scratch, selecting and combining all the individual parts for sound and color.

To complete the picture, there are also high-quality guitar companies, which emphasize their extensive use of machines, explaining that they permit greater precision and consistency than human hands.

Concert guitars, student guitars?

Real *concert guitars* are made by master luthiers. The word 'real' has been added because some budget brands use the name 'concert guitars' for their cheapest models. Rather deceptive, the more so because there are handmade *student guitars* that can easily cost a grand or more…

A good time
In the end you should buy the guitar that sounds and plays best for the price you're willing and able to pay. Some good news? In the lower and middle price ranges especially, quality has gone up and prices haven't. Whether a guitar is described as a handmade, concert or student guitar is less important. What the audience mainly hears are the notes you play, hardly anybody can hear or see the difference between a super-expensive instrument and something more affordable. What people *do* see is that you're having a good time on stage, and buying the right guitar will definitely help you in that.

THE STORE
The more guitars there are in stock, the harder it is to choose. On the other hand, as selecting guitars is largely a matter of comparing them, a wide selection is exactly what you need. It's equally important to find salespeople who enjoy their work and know what they're talking about. One more tip: Visit several music stores, and talk to a variety of salespeople, as they all have their own 'sound' too.

Time
Finally, take your time when buying an instrument – you'll have to live with it for years. On the other hand, you might end up buying that one guitar you liked straightaway, after just the first few notes.

Buying online
You can also buy musical instruments online or by mail-order. This makes it impossible to compare instruments, of course, but most online and mail-order companies offer a return service for most or all of their products: If you're not happy with it, you can return it within a certain period of time. Of course the instrument should be in new condition when you send it back.

USED GUITARS
A used guitar often costs half to two-thirds of its original price. For that kind of money it should be in good playing condition. Used guitars by well-known brands sell for

more than equally good guitars from unknown makes. You may want to take that into account when you buy a new one too.

Privately or in a store?

Purchasing a used instrument from a private individual may be cheaper than buying the same instrument from a store. One of the advantages of buying a used instrument in a store, though, is that you can go back if you have questions. Also, some music stores may offer you a limited warranty on your purchase. Another difference is that a good dealer won't usually ask an outrageous price, but a private seller might – because he doesn't know any better, or because he thinks that you don't.

MORE, MORE

If you want to know all there is to know, stock up on guitar magazines, which have reviews of the latest gear, and on all the brochures and catalogs you can find. Besides containing a wealth of information, the latter are designed to make you want to spend more than you have, or have in mind – so ask for a price list too. The Internet is another good source for up-to-date product information. And of course there are loads of other guitar books as well. You can find more about these resources beginning on page 122.

Fairs and conventions

One last tip: If a music trade show or convention is being held in your area, check it out. Besides lots of instruments you can try out and compare, you will also come across plenty of product specialists, as well as numerous fellow guitar players who are always a good source of information and inspiration.

TIPBOOK ACOUSTIC GUITAR

5. A GOOD GUITAR

Once you know what to look and listen out for, the differences between one guitar and another aren't that hard to spot. A chapter on the technical aspects of the instrument, from types of wood to sizes, the fingerboard, the neck, and even the frets. The sound is dealt with too, of course. Armed with this information, you're all set to buy the best guitar you can get.

The sound of a guitar depends to a large extent on the wood that has been used, and on the way it's been made. Chapters 7 and 8 are dedicated to the strings, which also play a major role.

Who's playing it

What a guitar sounds like also depends on who's playing it. If you haven't been playing that long, you won't be able to get the most out of an instrument.
If you really want to know what a guitar can sound like, have a good player play it – and that could well be the salesperson.

Look or listen

This chapter starts with a closer look at the instrument. If you want to choose one by using your ears only, then skip ahead to page 44.

Zippers and buckles

One more tip before you start play-testing guitars: Always be careful not to scratch the varnish with buckles, zippers, buttons, and bracelets.

Finishes

Most classical guitars look pretty much alike, whereas steel-string guitars offer more variety in terms of appearance. Besides variations in the size and color of the bodies, you'll also find different types of varnish (high-gloss, silky gloss or matte, for instance) and a wide range of pickguard, head, and bridge designs.

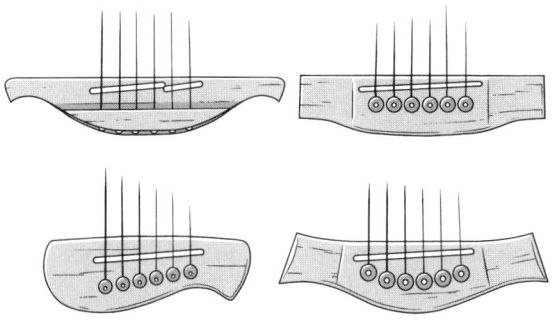

... a wide variety of bridge designs.

Varnish

Color is a matter of taste; the quality of the varnish isn't. Check, for example, that it has been applied evenly, and that there aren't any bubbles, stripes or drips. Look at the reflection too. If the guitar has a (silky) gloss varnish, the shine will tell you how well the various coats have been polished. Thick coats of varnish slow down the vibrations of the soundboard, restricting the instrument's sound.

Types of varnish

Until the 1970s, guitars were often finished with cellulose varnish, made of natural materials that are said to allow the wood to breathe. This type of varnish also makes it easier to make repairs without scarring the instrument. Today cellulose varnish is used only on some expensive guitars. The majority of instruments are finished with a synthetic-based varnish (*e.g.*, polyurethane); alcohol-based and water-based varnishes are also used.

Inlay

Classical guitars often have more intricately worked rosettes than steel-string instruments. Some cheap instruments have the rosette glued on, rather than inlaid.

The markers on the fingerboards of steel-string guitars vary from simple dots to elaborate abalone (mother-of-pearl) inlays.

THE BODY
A guitar's sound is, to a significant degree, determined by the body. By its size, for one thing, at least when it comes to steel-string guitars; classical guitars are pretty much all the same size.

Classical guitars
The dimensions of different classical guitars vary hardly at all. That goes both for the size of the body and for the so-called *speaking length* of the strings, measured from the nut to the saddle. This *scale* (see page 39) is usually a little over 25.5".

For children...
Smaller designs do exist, however. For younger children there are ¾- and ½-size guitars, with scales of around 24" (61 cm) and 23" (58 cm), respectively; even smaller models are available too. They are often tuned a bit higher; with a standard tuning, string tension would be too low.

... and for ladies
For female players there are so-called señorita guitars with a slightly diminished scale and a narrower neck. Other small nylon-string instruments are used mainly for specific styles of music; please refer to Chapter 13 for more information.

Steel-string guitars
Steel-string guitars come in all kinds of sizes. The basic rule is very simple: A bigger body gives you a bigger sound. To put it another way, you'll get more volume, a broader, richer, deeper sound, and more low-end.

Dreadnought and Jumbo
Two popular, large steel-string models are the Dreadnought, with an almost rectangular body shape, and the Jumbo. A Jumbo is much wider than a Dreadnought at the lower bout, but much narrower at the waist. The resulting

rounded shape is reflected in the sound of the instrument, which is often described as being a bit 'rounder' than that of the average Dreadnought.

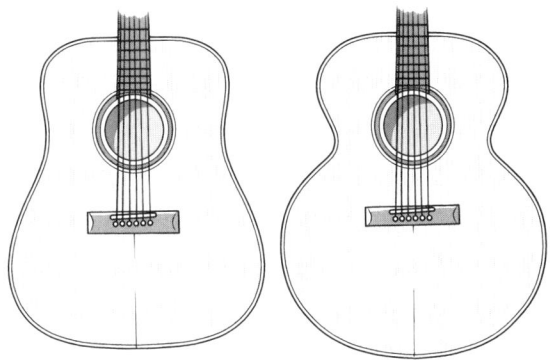

A Dreadnought and a Jumbo.

(Grand) Auditorium and (Grand) Concert
Another model is the Grand Auditorium, which is sometimes referred to as small Jumbo. This mid-size guitar is one of the most versatile instruments around. Just a bit smaller is the Auditorium, a size also known as Triple-0 or 000. The two smallest standard steel-string guitars are the Concert and the Grand Concert. There's more about all these instruments in Chapter 13.

Strumming and picking   Tipcode AGTR-004 and AGTR-005
The big, broad sound of a big steel-string guitar makes it very suitable for strumming. Guitars with smaller bodies are often used for *fingerpicking*; the thumb plays the bass, while the other fingers play the melody. You literally 'pick' the strings, in a way similar to the classical guitar technique.

Volume or control
Bigger guitars are also used in situations where plenty of volume is needed – usually live performances. In the studio however, a smaller guitar will often give better results: It's easier to control the sound, and loudness is not required.

Fiberglass body
Ovation was the first brand to introduce a guitar with a round, fiberglass back, appropriately named the *roundback*.

There are roundbacks with nylon and steel strings, with deep and shallow bodies, and also with bodies made of other materials. Roundbacks have a very specific sound, and they're almost always acoustic/electric instruments.

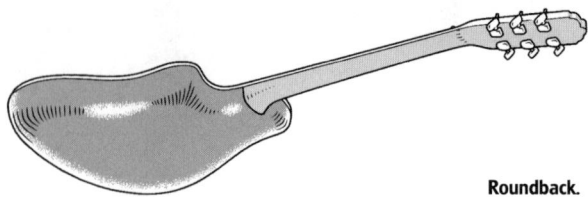

Roundback.

Cutaway

A so-called cutaway makes it easier to play the highest frets. Some brands offer certain models with or without a cutaway. Whether or not the difference can be heard has been debated for years. Some say the treble section sounds a bit brighter, due to the fact that the soundboard is smaller and therefore stiffer in that area; others feel that this fact actually reduces the trebles – and those are just two examples of the differences of opinion that exist, so listen and decide for yourself. A tip: The difference between two identical non-cutaway guitars can easily be bigger than the difference between a guitar with a cutaway and one without.

Florentine and Venetian

Cutaways are most common on steel-string guitars, but you may also find them on nylon-string models. They come in different shapes. The ones that end in a sharp point are known as Florentine cutaways, as opposed to the Venetian version, which has a rounded shape.

Florentine cutaway.

Venetian cutaway.

Guitar strap

If you play standing up as well, don't just try the guitar out sitting down. Strangely, most steel-string guitars have only one button to attach the strap to, at the tail. The other end of the strap is then attached to the head, using the lace that comes with the strap. Knot the lace around the head under the strings, just below the tuning machines of the E-strings. Never attach the strap to the tuning machine itself, as you can easily bend it. A tip: A second *strap button* can be screwed into the heel. Another tip: Have a specialized technician do that for you. A third tip: Classical guitars are not supposed to have strap buttons.

TOP AND INSIDE

The strings make the top vibrate, and those vibrations largely determine the sound of a guitar. This is what makes the top or *face* one of the most important parts of the instrument – and it also explains why it's known as the soundboard.

Solid

Guitars have either a *solid* or a *laminated top*. A solid top usually consists of a single piece of wood that has been split into two parts, much like an open book – hence the name *bookmatched* top.

Laminated

A laminated top, usually found on cheaper guitars, is made of plywood – a number of thin plies of wood that are glued together.

Better response
A solid-top guitar responds better to how loudly or how softly you play, or to how you strike the string (nails or pick) and where (at the bridge or at the neck), for example. Guitars with laminated tops often seem to have a bit less life to them, producing a shallower and less dynamic sound.

Solid-top classical guitars usually start around two to three hundred dollars. Steel-string guitars with a solid top are often a bit more expensive.

Always?
Tip: A solid-top instrument won't always sound better than one with a laminated top. There are instruments around which have laminated tops but still sound good, and there are guitars with solid tops that you're better off not buying.

The edge of the soundhole
A solid top can be recognized by looking at the edge of the soundhole. If the wood grain of the top continues beyond the edge, then you're looking at solid wood.

Fine, even grains
The quality of the wood itself is important too, as well as the way it has been sawed, the thickness, the structure, and so on. Top-of-the-range instruments often have thin soundboards, with a fine, even grain and a uniform hue – but there are top-of-the-range instruments that look nothing like that at all.

Slightly convex
While you're looking at the top, also look at it sideways. A good top is often slightly convex, though this will hardly be visible. A guitar with an obviously convex top is probably better left well alone, and the same goes for an instrument with a sagging, concave top.

Cedar or spruce
Most guitar tops are made of either cedar or spruce. Both are conifers, yet they have different characteristics. They also look different; cedar is usually brown, while spruce is much lighter, almost white in color.

How they sound
Most guitarists find the sound of a guitar with a cedar top a bit warmer, deeper, and rounder, while spruce tops are often said to sound a little brighter. Don't be surprised, however, if you hear an expert stating the opposite. Spruce is more commonly used for steel-string guitars and flamenco guitars, which need a fiercer type of sound. The American or Canadian Sitka spruce is especially popular among steel-string guitar luthiers. Cedar is more often used for classical guitars, though other woods such as the European Alpine spruce may also be used.

No two trees
Of course, one spruce or cedar top isn't identical to the next, just as no two trees are quite the same, and indeed just as the same tree can yield woods of a higher and a lesser quality. Also, wood can differ in the way it has been cured before being used. The moral? The sound is more important than the actual type of wood used.

Back and sides
The back and the sides are less important than the top. To prove that, the well-known luthier Torres (see page 95) is said to have built a guitar with a back and sides of papier-mâché. He told no one, played it, and everybody loved it... On the other hand, there are guitarists who say they can even hear the difference between a two- and a three-part back.

Laminated or solid
Most guitars have laminated backs and sides, but instruments with a body made entirely of solid wood are also available, for prices under – and well over – a thousand dollars.

Wood type
Mahogany is often used for the backs and sides of less expensive guitars. A colored varnish may be used to make it look like the more expensive (Rio) rosewood you find on better guitars. Other types of wood commonly used include maple and – in the higher price ranges – walnut or koa.

Size and material
The type of wood used may also depend on the size of the

guitar. Some makers use maple for their larger models, for instance, because this hard type of wood adds some brightness to these bassier-sounding instruments – the harder the wood, the brighter the tone will be. Softer woods make for a mellower sound.

Different materials
Some makers employ entirely different materials for their instruments, such as bamboo rather than wood. There are guitars made entirely of graphite, and instruments with a one-piece, plastic bracing system.

The inside too
Check the body, both inside and out, to see how well it has been finished. If you find gaps or big lumps of glue or varnish, it might give you cause to wonder if enough attention has been paid to the rest of the guitar. Also check that the neck and fingerboard connect seamlessly to the body, and that no craftsman's hand slipped while working with a file or a chisel. A high level of workmanship doesn't in itself guarantee a great-sounding guitar. Conversely, there are guitars that don't look good but sound wonderful. More often, though, the workmanship does tell you something about the all-around quality of the instrument you're looking at.

Bracing
Everything that's attached to the top determines how it vibrates. That, in turn, largely determines the sound of the guitar. A luthier can control the sound by varying the bracing pattern, for example, but also by using thinner, wider, higher, flatter, or scalloped braces. Each luthier has his own bracing 'recipe'.

Not all guitars have only one soundhole (Ovation).

Soundhole
Similarly, the sound of a guitar can be influenced by the size and position of the soundhole. Some guitars even have unusually shaped soundholes, or more than one.

GOOD NECK, GOOD FINGERBOARD
The neck and fingerboard are important to how a guitar plays and feels. To some extent, they help determine the sound as well.

Hard is brighter
The fingerboard is made of a hard type of wood. On less expensive guitars it's usually rosewood, with a dark-brown look; almost-black ebony is a popular choice for expensive guitars, being harder. The harder the wood of the fingerboard, the brighter and more direct the tone can be, and the fingerboard may have a smoother feel to it. There must not be any knots or cracks in the fingerboard.

Straight neck
The neck must be perfectly straight; it may not curve to the left or right. Check the neck by looking downwards from the head toward the body along the side of the fingerboard. You can check that the neck isn't twisted at the same time.

Intonation
At the twelfth fret, the strings should sound exactly one octave higher than when they are open – *i.e.*, when you don't fret them. If they do not, your guitar has bad intonation.

Harmonics Tipcode AGTR-006
Here's how you check this. Place a finger very lightly on the thick E-string, exactly above the twelfth fret, barely touching it, and then strike the string pretty hard, close to the bridge. What you'll hear – possibly only after some practice – is a high, thinnish tone, known as a *harmonic*, *overtone* or *flageolet*. Now press the same string to the twelfth fret, as you would in normal playing; you should get exactly the same pitch. Check the other strings in the same way.

Not easy
At first, it may not be that easy to hear whether a harmonic sounds too high, too low or just right. An electronic tuner (see page 81) can help, if it's a really good one, but an experienced guitarist may be even more effective.

A different pitch
If the intonation is off, you'll have problems when playing with other musicians; your high notes will have a slightly different pitch than theirs. The higher the fret you're playing, the more out of tune you will be. Another problem? On a guitar like this your ears slowly get used to the wrong pitches. You may not be too troubled by it until you switch to a good guitar, which can then sound out of tune, to you…

Decent strings
Some cheap guitars are sold with strings that simply don't allow for proper intonation – even on a perfect guitar. A set of decent strings solves the problem, improving your sound as well for less than ten dollars.

Dead spots
Another test is checking the instrument for *dead spots*. Play all the strings at all of the frets and listen for positions where a string sounds noticeably shorter, drier or softer.

Rattles
While you're at it, also check for rattles and buzzing sounds – especially on used guitars. Some unwanted noises may be noticeable only at certain pitches. Harmonics, which you can also play at a number of other frets (the fifth and the seventh, for example), can sometimes make otherwise inaudible sounds stand out. Another test? Gently tap the body with a fingertip or a knuckle and listen, or carefully shake the guitar. If you want to know more about rattles and buzzes, and their possible causes, check out pages 47–48.

Concave neck
A guitar neck should be slightly concave from the head to the body. To check this, press the low E-string simultaneously at both the first and the fifteenth fret. The

middle of the string should now be floating just a little above the frets in the middle of the neck. If not, you've got a flat neck, or even a convex one, which may result in strings rattling against the frets. If there's more than about $1/32"$ (1 mm) between the string and the frets, the neck is too concave, making the guitar harder to play.

A third hand
If you're unable to see whether the string touches the frets, you'll need a third hand to strike it, so ask someone else to play the string while you hold it. If the string sounds, everything's okay.

Adjustable necks
The necks of most steel-string guitars can be adjusted with the built-in truss rod. Classical guitars are not adjustable in this way.

MORE ABOUT NECKS
Steel-string guitars come with a wide variety of necks. There's also plenty to tell about the necks of classical guitars.

Broad
Classical guitars have pretty wide fingerboards, measuring a little over two inches (5 cm) at the nut. The strings are quite widely spaced, to allow for the techniques used in classical guitar music. When you're just starting out, a slightly narrower, thinner neck will be easier to play, but there aren't too many options to choose from.

Your thumb   Tipcode AGTR-007
Proper classical guitar technique requires you to rest the thumb of your left hand somewhere in the middle of the back of the neck. This makes it easier to stop the strings with the tips of your fingers, and it allows you to spread your fingers as widely as possible. The neck has been designed for this purpose.

Profile
The necks of many steel-string guitars, on the other hand, are designed to make playing chords easier. Most players

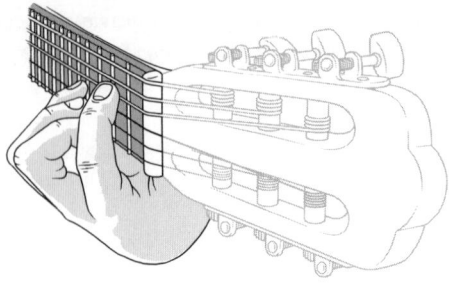

Classical left-hand technique.

have their thumbs higher on the back of the neck, just like electric-guitar players usually do.

D, C and V

The profile of a neck is hard to put into words. Using letters is easier; a neck with a D-profile has a rather flat back, while the letter C indicates a rounder profile. Necks with a 'sharper' V-profile are mainly used by guitarists who fret the sixth string, or even the fifth string, with their left thumb. This slightly pointed profile allows your thumb to fit more easily around it. Fingerpickers tend to like this type of neck too. Most of them also prefer the slightly wider string spacing that comes with a broader neck.

Radius

Steel-string guitars, like most electric guitars, have fingerboards that are a bit higher underneath the middle strings and gently slope down toward the thin and thick strings. This rounding, called *radius* or *camber*, makes it easier to finger chords.

Flat or round?

The radius is expressed in inches. The higher the number, the flatter the fingerboard. Most steel-string guitars have a radius of twelve inches. A neck with a *compound radius* is a bit rounder at the nut than at the last fret.

Neck widths

There's more variation in the width of the neck among steel-string guitars than among classical guitars. The necks are usually between 1 $^{11}/_{16}$" and 1 $^{13}/_{16}$" wide at the nut (42-46 mm), getting wider toward the neck and usually ending up slightly over 2" (5 cm). If you play mainly chords, a narrower fingerboard makes things easier. For other playing techniques, like fingerpicking, a lot of guitarists prefer a wider neck.

THE SCALE

When an open string is struck, it vibrates between the nut and the saddle. This vibrating part is called the *speaking length* of the string. This equals the *scale* of the guitar, which is used to indicate its size. On steel-string guitars the scale usually varies from a little under 25" to about 26" (62.5–66 cm). Most classical guitars have a scale of a little over 25.5" (65 cm).

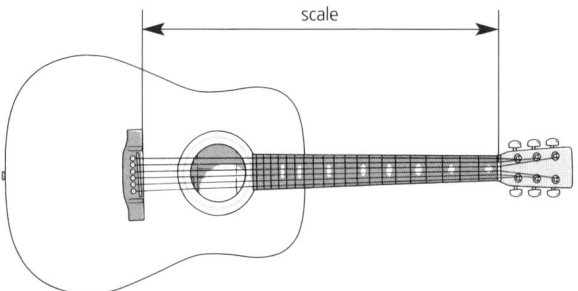

The scale is the length of the strings measured from the saddle to the nut.

Tighter

The longer the scale, the further apart the frets will be, so the more you have to spread your fingers. Also, the strings have to be wound a little tighter to sound the same pitch. This increased tension helps produce a broader, fuller sound and a little more volume. Fingerpicking guitarists often choose long-scale guitars.

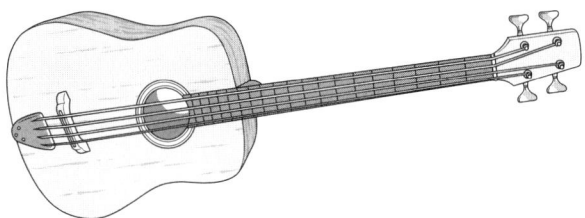

Acoustic bass guitars have longer scales.

Acoustic bass guitars
Most acoustic bass guitars have four strings, each tuned one octave below the equivalent (lowest-sounding) four strings of a 'regular' guitar. Short strings can't go that low and still sound good, so that's why bass guitars have much longer scales, up to around 34" (86 cm).

Decide for yourself
Guitarists with big hands often – but not always – prefer a thick neck to a slim one, and vice versa. Some guitarists would rather play on a flat, thick neck with a round fingerboard. Other guitarists prefer a round, slim neck with a flatter fingerboard. Sometimes these choices are based on the music you play, and sometimes they're not. The message: Watch and listen to what other guitarists are doing, but decide for yourself what suits you best.

Fourteen-fret and twelve-fret necks
Most steel-string guitars have a fourteen-fret neck, meaning that the body starts at the fourteenth fret. These necks seem to be longer than twelve-fret necks, but that's not the difference. In fact, the difference lies in the soundbox: Guitars with a twelve-fret neck have a longer soundbox, 'reaching out' to the twelfth fret, as it were. This can make for a slightly bigger, rounder sound, with the drawback that it's harder to play the highest positions. Another difference: The necks of twelve-fret models are often a bit wider.

A choice of necks
You've found a great guitar, but you're not happy about the neck? Usually, that would be a problem, but some expensive series come with a choice of necks, as well as a choice of different position markers and other inlays.

ACTION
The action of a guitar refers to the distance between the strings and the fingerboard. A guitar with a high action has its strings rather high above the fingerboard, and vice versa.

Too high, too low
The higher the action, the heavier the guitar will play; you have to press the strings down quite far before they touch

the frets. If the action is too low, the strings will rattle against the frets. Flamenco guitarists often produce that rattling sound intentionally, by playing with a very low action and fiercely attacking the strings with their nails.

From high to low
On new guitars the action is more often on the high than on the low side. That makes sense, as it's easier to lower a high action than it is to raise a low one. An action that's too high can also be remedied temporarily – when you're trying out guitars, for instance.

A capo
A guitar with a very high action is hard to judge. The temporary solution? A *capo*, which is a clamp that you can mount anywhere on the neck. Capos are really designed to raise the pitch of the guitar in half steps (see page 83), but they can also be used to temporarily lower the action. For that purpose, you capo the first fret. This will make the guitar sound a half-tone (half-step) higher, but what really counts at this stage is that it's comfortable to play.

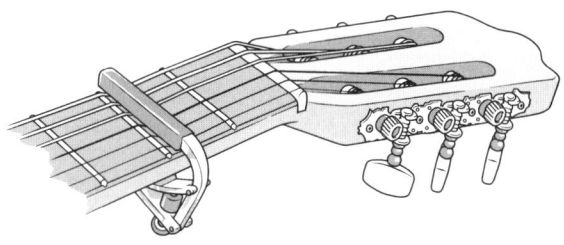

A capo, shown here in the second position. Like most other models, this capo can also be mounted the other way around.

Adjusting the action
Of course you can't leave the capo on the guitar forever, and you won't need to either. A technician can adjust the action by lowering the nut or the saddle, or, conversely, by replacing them with taller models. On steel-string guitars, the truss rod may have to be adjusted as well.

Nylon-string action
A classical guitar is considered to have a low action if the distance between the twelfth fret and the bottom of the

thick E-string is about 9/64" (3.5 mm) or less. If there's more than about 3/16" (4.75 mm) clearance, the action is considered high – but there are great classical guitars with an action of more than 4/16" (6.35 mm). The action on the low E-string is usually a bit higher than on the high E-string; thick strings need more space to move. If the overall action is too low, the sound may suffer.

Steel-string action
Steel-string guitars have a lower overall action. Usually there's about 1/16" under the high E (1.5 mm) and a bit more under the low E (5/64" or 2 mm). If you use a slide, you'll probably want a higher action.

METAL AND BONE
The main non-wood parts of a guitar are the tuners, the frets, the nut, and the saddle. Even these small elements contribute to the instrument's quality, playability, and appearance.

Tuning machines
Tuning machines – also known as *machine heads*, *tuning heads* or *tuning gears* – should wind easily and smoothly, have no backlash, and produce no buzzes or rattles. On classical guitars they're always open, while most steel-string guitars have enclosed tuners, encased by a metal housing. These sealed tuners are usually self-lubricating; there's no need to oil them.

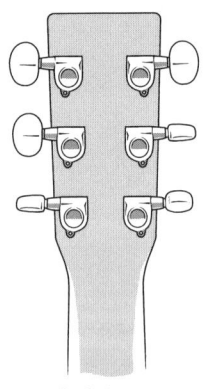

Sealed tuners on a steel-string guitar.

Gear ratios
Tuning machines can also differ in what 'gear' they're in. If you have 10:1 tuners, the posts that wind the string turn around once for every ten times you turn the key.
Tuning is easier and more precise with 14:1 or even 16:1 tuners. And if you've found a great guitar, but you're not happy about the tuning machines, they can be easily replaced.

Gold-plated

Many steel-string guitars have gold-colored tuning machines instead of chrome-plated ones. That gold color may actually be brass, but there are also gold-plated tuning machines, and they're not as expensive as you might think.

Frets

Smooth and well-finished frets make for an easy-playing guitar that feels good in your hands. You may come across frets that are a little too short, resulting in E-strings that slip off of the fingerboard. If they're too long they jut out from the neck, which may indicate that the guitar has been stored in too dry an environment (see pages 90–91).

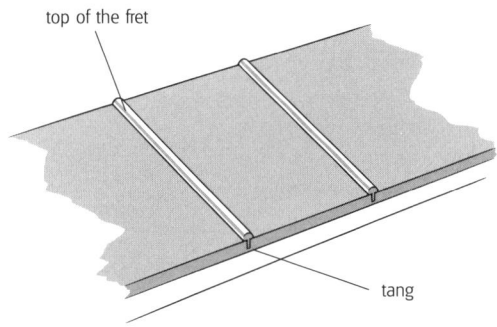

Edgier frets, edgier sound

And yes, even frets influence the sound of an instrument. Frets with an edgier top make for an 'edgier' sound, while rounder frets can make the sound, you got it, a little rounder.

Fretless basses

There are acoustic bass guitars that have a fretless neck, just like a double bass. Their timbre is described as having a 'singing' quality, and there's less attack in the sound. In order to play in tune, you have to stop the strings in exactly the right place, rather than some place in between two frets. This is what makes playing fretless instruments quite a bit harder than fretted ones. Fretless guitars are very rare, but they do exist.

Two octaves

Nylon-string guitars usually have eighteen or nineteen frets. In addition, they sometimes have one or two half-frets beside the soundhole, for the very highest notes. Steel-string guitars usually have twenty frets. On some guitars you'll find a twenty-fourth fret, for the high E and B-strings. This allows you to play two octaves on those strings – but it isn't easy.

Bridge saddle and nut
Most bridge saddles and nuts are made of a hard synthetic material designed to pass on the vibrations of the strings to the guitar as well as possible. They used to be made of ivory, but that's no longer allowed. Bone nuts and saddles may be found on more expensive guitars.

Compensated saddles
Steel-string guitars often have a *compensated* saddle; the saddle is not at a 90º angle to the strings, as it is on most classical guitars. Compensated saddles are designed to improve a guitar's intonation, making it sound in tune in each and every position. Some saddles even consist of two or more parts, for the same reason.

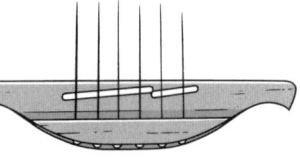

A compensated saddle.

The nut
If you're trying a guitar out and the strings keep getting stuck while you're tuning, the grooves in the nut might be too narrow. A temporary solution? Repeatedly press the string you're tuning just behind the nut. The permanent solution is to have the nut adjusted or replaced.

WHAT TO LISTEN FOR
Besides dead spots and poor intonation, there's a lot more to listen for. Here are some more tips for judging guitars with your ears.

A wall works well
When you're playing, you don't hear the same sound as your audience does. You can come close, though. Just sit down facing a wall so that the sound of the guitar bounces back to you. Another solution? Ask the salesperson to play

a few different guitars, or take somebody with you who can play them for you. A little distance may help you to judge the sound and the character of the instrument better.

Balanced
A good guitar is well-balanced in terms of volume, tone, and sustain. The low strings shouldn't be louder than the high ones, nor the other way around. Because they're wound, the low strings not only sound lower than the high ones, they also sound different. They shouldn't sound too different, however.

The third string
On nylon-string guitars, the third string (G) often deviates. Being the heaviest plain string, it sounds much less bright than the D, which is the thinnest wound string. Some strings and string sets have been designed to reduce this effect (see pages 56–57).

Sustain
As for the sustain, the thin strings don't sustain as long as the thick ones, and in higher positions the sustain will get shorter – but it should be balanced, and never get too short.

Dynamics
Something else to listen to is a guitar's range from loud to soft: the dynamics. The guitar should have a beautiful, full tone even at its quietest, and it should sound just as good when you play it really loud. The best check? Play it the way you're going to play it – but do remember that it's not yours yet.

Taste
Apart from that, what makes a good sound is mainly a matter of taste, and the style of music you're going to use the guitar for. Some ideas? You could go for a bright sound, or you may prefer something warmer. The heavy basses that one player wants may sound too boomy to another. Some guitars have a very transparent sound; when you play a chord, you can hear every single string separately. Other instruments have a thicker, heavier, solid type of sound.

Transparent
A guitar with a transparent sound will often sound bright too, with lots of highs. A nasal-sounding guitar may sound blocked in one way, but it may offer the perfect timbre for some situations – and it doesn't have to be the same thing as a guitar without much high end, because a sound like that could be just as well described as bass-like, warm, round, thick, or fat.

Deep or shallow
One guitar might have a deep, rich sound, while another may tend to a shallower sound, being less articulate and less dynamic. A shallow sound may not be unpleasant at first, but it can become boring after a while.

What you like
Another point to bear in mind is that when two people listen to the same guitar, they'll probably use different words to describe what they hear. What one finds harsh (in other words, unpleasant), another may describe as bright (in other words, pleasant), and what's warm to one ear sounds dull to another. It all depends on what you like – and the words you use to describe it.

Three
When you're trying to choose the best of a whole bunch of guitars, it's easy to get confused. A tip? Pick out three guitars, based on the salesperson's advice or your own ears. Play them. Then swap the one you like least for another instrument. Listen. And so on.

Don't look
When selecting the guitars you want to listen to, you'll almost automatically look at the price as well. Chances are that you will *hear* that price too. A solution? Let the salesperson hand you a number of guitars in your price range, one by one. Don't look. Just play them, one by one. And listen.

Turn around
If you've found a couple of guitars that feel good and play well, and you intend to choose between them on the basis of their sound, ask someone to play the same piece of

music on each guitar. If you really want to go only for the sound, and not for the looks, turn around so that you can't see which guitar is being played.

Never the same
Just as no two trees are ever the same, you'll never find two guitars that sound exactly alike. Not even if they're of the same brand and the same series, and built the same day by the same person. So it's advisable to always play the guitar you're going to buy, and to buy the guitar which you played, instead of an 'identical' one from the stockroom.

Longer
A guitar often starts to sound its best after you've played it for fifteen or twenty minutes. Only then does the instrument really open up, as some would say. Another explanation is that it takes you about twenty minutes to get to know a guitar to the point where you can make it sound better…

Acoustic/electric
Many acoustic/electric guitars are 'regular' guitars with a built-in pickup, and judging their acoustic properties is not any different from what you've just read.

USED INSTRUMENTS
Used guitars require the same tests and checks as new ones, but there are a few things that need extra attention.
- Check the body, the neck, and the fingerboard for **cracks and other damage**.
- Damage is caused not only by bumps and falls, but also by dry air or by sudden changes in **air humidity** (see page 90–92).
- **Small cracks in the varnish** may indicate that a guitar has been stored in a very dry environment, just like frets that jut out from the neck.
- Also pay attention to **seams and joints**, for example between fingerboard and body.
- Listen for things you don't want to hear. Some **rattles or buzzes** may be easily corrected, perhaps by fastening a strap button, replacing a string whose winding has come undone, or, on a classical guitar, cutting a piece of string

CHAPTER 5

that is buzzing against the top, right behind the bridge. If a string is broken, its tuning machine won't be silent.
- There are other **sounds** you won't be able to get rid of, or you'll need to have them repaired by a specialist. A loose brace, for example. More examples? A pickguard that's come loose, an invisible crack in the body, a loose nut, or a screw on a tuner…
- **Worn-out frets** can make your strings buzz, and they hamper string-bending. Frets can be replaced or refinished.

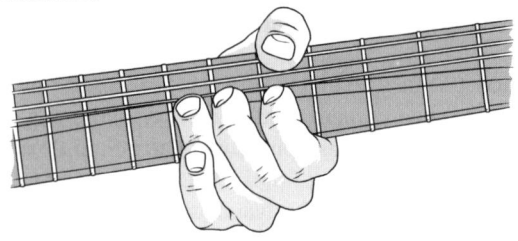

Bending strings; a tough job with worn-out frets.

- Poor intonation may be the result of **an old set of strings**.
- The tiniest drop of oil can makes **tuning machines** run smoothly again. Inferior or old ones can be replaced, if the guitar is worth it.
- A good used guitar can last **years and years** more.
- On acoustic/electric guitars, check to see if all the **controls** are working well, and make sure they don't creak. Creaking is often easily solved with contact spray, but even then you have to know what you're doing.
- A final tip, to underline an earlier point: **Take somebody along** who knows about guitars, especially if you're buying from a private seller.

Vintage instruments

Vintage violins can cost well over a million dollars. Guitars have yet to become that expensive, but there are vintage instruments that cost at least as much as new ones of similar quality. This has to do with older instruments being rare, and partly with the fact that the sound of a good guitar may well improve with age.

6. ACOUSTIC/ELECTRIC GUITARS

Only if it's really quiet, like at a classical guitar concert, will the sound of an acoustic guitar be loud enough to fill a concert hall. Quite often, you'll need a little more volume – or a lot more. That's where acoustic/electric guitars come in – acoustic guitars that you can hook up directly to an amplifier.

Most acoustic/electric guitars don't look any different from a regular steel-string guitar – and they're usually the same instruments, apart from the built-in electronics.

Control panel
You can recognize most acoustic/electrics by the small control panel for the preamplifier, located on the left upper bout.

Pickup
The pickup or *transducer* is usually a *piezo pickup* – a very thin, small strip which can be hidden under the bridge saddle.

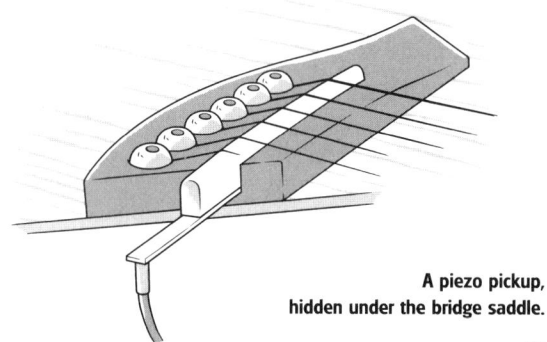

A piezo pickup, hidden under the bridge saddle.

Input jack
The cable is plugged in the input jack, located in the strap button at the tail of the instrument.

Prices
Acoustic/electric guitars, with either steel or nylon strings, come in a wide variety of prices. The cheapest models start as low as two hundred fifty or three hundred dollars. More money may buy you a better guitar, a better pickup/preamp combination, or both. Quite a few brands offer you a choice of systems by different makers.

A microphone
Some systems feature both a piezo pickup and a small microphone to round off the sound. The sound of a piezo pickup is usually said to be rather clean; the microphone, clipped on the edge of the soundhole or mounted inside, provides a more natural, warm sound. With such systems, the balance between the two can usually be adjusted: more piezo if feedback (see below) is a problem, more microphone if it's not, for instance.

Microphone under the bridge
As an alternative to piezo pickups, there are also microphones which can be installed under the bridge saddle, similar to a piezo.

Shallow bodies
Another category of acoustic/electrics are the instruments, mostly nylon-strung, that are built solely for amplified playing. They often have a shallow body that hardly, if at all, acts as a soundbox, and they may have some type of grill rather than a conventional soundhole.

Feedback problems and solutions
Acoustic/electric guitars are notorious for causing *feedback*; the loud *skreee* you also hear if you accidentally point a microphone at a loudspeaker. The deeper and larger the guitar's body and the louder you play, the more likely you are to have feedback problems. Two common solutions? The first is a *notch filter*, which may be found on the preamp or on the external amp. It combats feedback by filtering the relevant frequency out of the sound. The

second is simply to close the soundhole with a rubber disc, known as a *feedback buster* or some such name. Then there are wooden soundhole covers, some with intricate carvings.

Volume and tone

The control panel of an acoustic/electric usually features both volume and tone controls, the latter often separated into high (treble) and low (bass) – just like a home stereo amplifier. Some preamps offer more extensive tone controls (an *equalizer* or *EQ*), or allow you to adjust the brilliance of the sound.

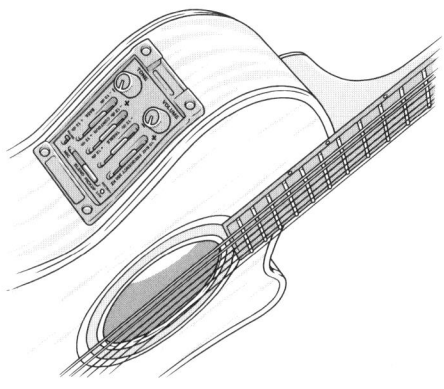

A nylon-string acoustic/electric with a shallow body.

Effects and tuners

Other preamplifiers also offer effects. Most commonly a reverb, adding depth and space to the sound, but there are preamps with a built-in delay, chorus, and other effects. Some come with user presets to memorize various settings, and built-in electronic tuners are no longer rare.

Battery check

The preamp is usually powered by a 9-volt battery. A check light on the control panel warns you when the power runs low. You'll hear that as well, as the sound will get progressively worse. In most systems the battery will last at least five hundred to a thousand hours, or even longer. Tip: Always unplug the instrument as soon as you stop playing. This switches the preamp off, extending the life of the battery.

Invisible

Not all preamps have a control panel on board. Some systems have the preamp built in a small tube, attached to the input jack/strap button. One major advantage is that they don't require a hole to be made in the side of your instrument. The battery is mounted in a small clamp close to the soundhole. Unwinding the strings provides enough space to replace it.

Retrofitting

Pickups and preamps can be retrofit as well – preferably by a specialized technician. A pickup that's not properly installed may cause feedback problems, for one thing. The prices of pickups and preamps vary a lot, as does the cost of having them built in. If you want really good results, count on spending about two to three hundred dollars or more, everything included. Some of the better known brands in this area are Ashworth, B-Band, EMG, EPM, Fishman, Highlander, Lace, L.R. Baggs, and Seymour Duncan.

Which guitar?

Basically you can turn any guitar into an acoustic/electric, but many guitarists prefer a model with a body that's not too big, in order to minimize feedback problems. The Grand Concert size is a popular choice.

Once in a while

If your guitar needs to be amplified just once in while, you can go for a magnetic pickup that can be mounted in the soundhole, using clips or clamps, or adhesive tape. Prices range from fifty dollars to four times as much, and more. But remember: Magnetic pickups don't respond to nylon strings. And whatever you do, don't replace your nylon strings with steel ones, as this will ruin the instrument.

Microphone

Regular microphones are usually used in studios. Onstage you risk feedback, and you'll have to keep your guitar very still, aiming the soundhole at the microphone at all times. A clip-on microphone, as described above, buys you the freedom to move around. There are also ultra-flat microphones that can be stuck onto or inside the body, so that no holes have to be drilled.

Acoustic amplifiers

Unlike amplifiers for electric guitars, which contribute a lot to the sound of the instrument, amps for acoustic guitars are supposed to only amplify the sound – to make it louder, not to change it. These special amps are known as *acoustic amplifiers*, contradictory as that may sound. Most well-known amplifier manufacturers offer one or more types.

Power ratings

The smallest acoustic amps have a power output of some 15 or 25 watts RMS, which is enough for only the very smallest venues. Need more power? Expect to pay some five or six hundred dollars for a decent amp of 40 to 50 watts. Prices, power output, sound quality, and features can only go up from there. If you play in a band with other amplified instruments, you'll soon be needing up to 100 watts or more, unless there's a PA system.

Combo

Acoustic amplifiers are usually *combo amplifiers* or *combos*, with one or more small loudspeakers (often only 5" or 8") and an amplifier all in one box. Some models come with a bigger speaker combined with a dedicated tweeter that looks like a small horn, for the highest frequencies. Each combo has its own sound, so always listen to a couple of them before buying one, and preferably use your own guitar to play-test them.

Effects

Most amps have one or more built-in effects. A reverb is a welcome addition, especially if you use the same amp for vocals as well; many amps feature a microphone input, since many guitar players sing too. Another popular built-in effect is *chorus*, which doubles the sound and gives it a fuller, more dynamic and spacious feel. These and other effects are also available in dedicated effects units for acoustic instruments.*

Buying tips

- Always listen to acoustic/electrics **unamplified** (even those with a shallow body) **as well as amplified**.

---

* Want to know more? Read Tipbook Amplifiers and Effects *(see page 128).*

- When you play the guitar amplified, does the sound only get louder or does the **tone** change as well?
- Acoustic/electric guitars often have a rather **low action and light strings**. Keep that in mind when you're trying them out.
- How sensitive is the guitar to **feedback**? It's easier to find that out when you compare a couple of guitars. Sit down with those guitars at different angles to the speakers – and don't open the amplifier up all the way…
- Check that the volume and tone controls work **evenly**, and across their entire range.
- Listen for **noise and hum**. If you hear any, the culprit may be the guitar, but it could also be the cable, the amp, or other electrical systems in the room.
- Check if **the battery** is easily replaceable.

7. STRINGS

A good set of strings will allow you to get the most out of your instrument. Strings affect both the sound and the feel of the guitar, and there's a wide variety to choose from. A chapter on plain and wound strings, low-tension and high-tension strings, and heavy and light strings.

Strings sound best when you fit them properly, and they'll sound good longer if you keep them clean. Chapter 8 deals with both subjects.

Crack
Steel strings put quite a lot of tension on your guitar – a force comparable to the weight of a fully-grown guitar player. Nylon-string guitars are designed to cope with about half that tension. If you put steel strings on a nylon-string guitar, the top may crack, the bridge may come loose, or the neck may warp, to name just a few of the risks. So don't do it.

Nylon on steel
Putting nylon strings on a steel-string guitar is not a good idea either. The posts are not designed for nylon strings, and the strings lack the amount of tension that you'd need to make the soundboard vibrate sufficiently. The result? Not much at all, really.

Which strings
The only way to find out exactly which brand or series of strings you like best on your guitar is to try them out. A knowledgeable salesperson may help you narrow down

the extensive choice somewhat. Describe the sound you're looking for, and he or she will be able to suggest a few types and brands that may match your taste.

Cheap strings
It has been said before: Cheap guitars often come with cheap strings. Any decent set of strings will noticeably improve the sound of the instrument, as well as its intonation.

NYLON STRINGS
Nylon strings are available in various tensions, windings, colors, types, and brands. Here are the basics.

Tensions
Most brands offer three choices when it comes to string tension, some four, and a few brands even more. Compared to normal- or low-tension strings, high tension strings feel a bit tighter and play a bit 'heavier', and the sound is a bit brighter and more articulate. Lower tension strings are easier to play, and they tend to produce a warmer, drier, less distinctive sound.

Wound strings
The three thickest strings consist of ultra-fine nylon wires that are twisted together (*floss nylon* or *multifilaments*) and wound with metal wire. The winding makes the strings heavier, which allows them to sound as low as they should while keeping a bright, tight sound. If you were to use plain nylon wire for these strings, they'd have to be really thick, resulting in a dull, weak, tubby tone.

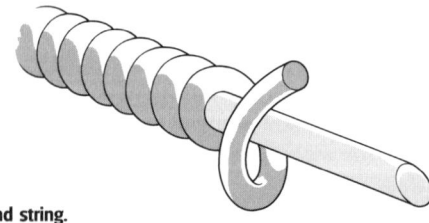

A wound string.

The third string
To an extent this is illustrated by the third string, the G. Being a bit on the heavy side for a plain nylon string, it tends

to sound a bit muddy or tubby compared to its wound neighbor, the D. To reduce this difference, some brands offer wound third strings, or they use a different type of nylon. Some sets come with two G-strings: a regular one, and one made of a different material, so you can compare the two.

Silver, bronze, or gold-plated
Most wound strings have a silver-plated brass winding, which allows a nice, bright tone. Bronze wound strings are often said to sound a bit warmer (if you like them) or less bright (if you don't). Strings with gold-plated brass windings sound good, but the brightness may not last that long, since gold is rather soft.

Clear, yellow, or black
Plain strings are usually made of clear transparent nylon, like fishing wire, but there are yellow and black ones too. Most experts say the color doesn't do anything to the sound; others believe that black strings sound a bit brighter – or darker…

Prices
A decent set of nylon strings costs about seven to ten dollars. A really good guitar will benefit from better strings, from ten dollars upwards. It may be worthwhile to try such a set, even if it is just for once. You won't know what you're missing if you don't.

A year or more
Even after a year or more, plain strings can still sound as if they were brand new. Eventually, though, you won't be able to tune them properly anymore and the intonation will be off (see page 35).

Wound strings
Wound strings don't keep their tone that long. Sweat attacks the windings and dirt can easily settle in the grooves between the windings, both resulting in a duller tone. How long that takes may depend on the quality of the strings, on how often you play, how well you look after your strings and, last but not least, on the acidity of your perspiration. The more acidic it is, the faster the sound will deteriorate.

How long
Depending on how much you play, how good your guitar is, and how good you want it to sound, you can change your strings every one or two months, every week, every day, or only when they break. The better your guitar and your playing, the sooner you'll hear a loss of brightness and tone. As a starting point: If you put on new strings after a month and you don't hear the difference, you may want to wait a little longer next time. If you hear a difference right away, consider changing strings more often.

Nine or seven in a set
Since wound strings lose their tone sooner, it makes sense to replace them more often than your plain ones. For this reason, some brands sell strings in sets of nine, doubling the three wound strings.
As the D-string, which is the thinnest wound string, wears down faster than the other strings, some sets are sold with two D-strings. Strings can be bought one at the time too, but that works out more expensive than buying them per set.

Brands
Some of the main nylon string brands are Aranjuez, Augustine, D'Addario, D'Aquisto, La Bella, GHS, Hannabach, Savarez, and Thomastik-Infeld.

STEEL STRINGS
Plain steel strings don't differ that much from one brand to the next. A possible exception is silver steel strings, which are said to sound a bit more, well, silvery. On steel-string guitars, the third string is usually wound. However, some players prefer a plain G, because it's easier to bend. Whereas nylon strings come in various tensions, steel strings come in different gauges, from light to heavy. The wound strings are of course available with various windings.

Bronze windings
The silver-plated windings that work so well on nylon strings are rarer on steel strings. A bronze winding, which is more popular, gives steel strings a bright, open sound.

Phosphor bronze
Strings with phosphor bronze windings are a popular alternative. Some guitarists feel they sound a bit brighter, others will tell you the opposite – the usual story among musicians. The only way to find out is to buy a set and try them on your own guitar; the sound of a set of strings depends on the guitar about as much as the other way around.

Comparing strings
There are lots of other variations, ranging from different windings to strings that combine silk and steel in the core. An effective and inexpensive way to compare strings? Replace one of the wound strings (the fourth or the fifth, preferably) with a string from the brand or series you want to judge. You can also fit a new E of one type of string and a new A of another type. Listen closely, and then replace with a new E of the latter type, and an A of the first type. This way, you compensate for misleading differences due to string thicknesses and pitches. Of course, there's no point comparing strings unless they're all new.

Various tensions
Steel strings come in various gauges. The main differences are shown below.

Four main differences between lighter and heavier gauge strings:

Lighter gauge strings	Heavier gauge strings
• sound 'lighter', edgier, and shorter	• sound 'heavier', fatter, and longer
• produce less volume	• produce more volume
• are easier to play	• make playing a bit heavier
• need to be tuned more often	• don't detune as fast
• break more easily	• last longer

One-hundredth of an inch
String gauges are expressed in fractions of an inch. When guitarists speak about the gauge of a set of strings, they always refer to the first string. In an 010-set, the first string measures 0.010", equaling 0.25 mm. Most steel-string guitar players opt for a set of 012-strings.

Getting used to it
Most electric guitar players use 010-sets, or even lighter

strings. Switching to an acoustic guitar with heavier gauge strings may take some getting used to. You can use 010s on a steel-string guitar, but most instruments will sound better with slightly heavier strings, which deliver more volume and a richer, broader tone. You could try a set of 011s before switching to 012, of course. The heaviest sets for steel-string guitars are 014.

Names
Some brands use names to indicate string gauges, often ranging from extra light (010) to heavy (014). The exact names and the gauges they refer to may vary per brand. The same goes for the precise gauges of the other strings in the set.

Times 4.5
The sixth string is usually around 4.5 times the gauge of the first one: sets range from 010 to 045, and from 012 to 054, for example.

Heavier strings, higher tension
The heavier the strings, the more tension they put on your instrument. Replacing your strings with heavier ones may therefore result in a higher action, because of the force they exert at the neck and the top. Of course that higher action can be lowered in turn (see pages 40–42 and 88).

Caught at the nut
The strings of a heavier set can get caught in the grooves of the nut, making it impossible to tune them properly. The solution is to have the nut replaced or to have the grooves adapted.

Sweat
How long a set of steel strings lasts depends on many things. You will have to change them more often than nylon strings, as steel strings are much more sensitive to sweat – especially if your sweat happens to be very acidic. As with nylon strings, the wound strings will usually lose their tone and brightness long before the plain ones.

Two weeks, two years…
Guitarists who want to keep their sound up to scratch

often change their strings every two weeks to two months. There are plenty of players, though, who put on a new set even more frequently. On the other hand, you can easily enjoy one and the same set for over two years – and you won't know what you've been missing until you install new steel, when everything will sound a whole lot brighter right away.

Can you hear it?
If you fit new strings after a month and you don't really hear a difference, you could try waiting a little longer the next time. If you do hear the difference, it might be worth changing them sooner next time.

Coating
Some brands make strings with a special coating, which reduces the effect of sweat and dirt, to extend the string's life expectancy. There are also various products available to treat strings for the same purpose yourself.

Prices and brands
A good set of steel strings costs around seven to ten dollars, but you may find cheaper strings that sound good and hold up well too. Good strings generally sound better, keep sounding good longer and last longer. A few well-known steel string brands are D'Addario, D'Aquisto, Dean Markley, DR, Ernie Ball, Gibson, GHS, Kyser, Martin, SIT, and Thomastik-Infeld.

8. CLEANING AND CHANGING STRINGS

To get the best out of your instrument, you'll need to pay some extra attention to your strings – and that doesn't take much time or effort. Keeping them clean and fitting them properly is basically all you need to do. Tuning tips follow in Chapter 9.

To get your strings to last as long as they can, you should take a closer look at your guitar too. First, the smoother the frets are, the longer your strings can last. Rough spots can be smoothed, very carefully, with some ultra-fine steel wool.

Nut and saddle

Second, excessive string wear can be the result of sharp edges at the nut or the saddle. It may pay to check these parts, especially if a certain string keeps breaking in the same place. As before, fine steel wool, or some ultra-fine sandpaper, will usually be all you need to smooth things down.

Elasticity

Even if you never play them, strings gradually lose their elasticity and the sound grows duller. Put on a new set, and the sound will suddenly be bright as can be.

Dust, dirt, grease...

Strings also lose their brightness because they are affected by airborne dust, dirt, grease, smoke, and moisture, as well as by whatever your fingers leave on them. Wound strings are especially sensitive to this kind of pollution, because they retain everything so well in their grooves. A guideline: When wound strings start losing their color, they are past their best. They may not break for another year, two years or more, but a new set will dramatically improve the sound of your instrument.

Cleaner and drier
An easy way to keep your strings as dry and clean as possible is to wash your hands and dry them well before playing, and to clean and dry the strings afterwards. Any type of lint-free cloth works well – an old T-shirt or a dishtowel, for instance. Clean the underside of the strings and the fingerboard, as you go along. Simply pull the cloth between the strings and the fingerboard, and run it up and down the neck a couple of times.

String cleaner
If you have particularly sweaty fingers, a special string cleaner may help. These cleaners also remove the dirt from the grooves of your wound strings. They're not expensive – just a couple of dollars buys you a bottle that'll last a long time.

Smoother strings
Other products make your strings feel a little smoother, and they often help to repel dirt as well. Each manufacturer dreams up its own product name, such as Finger-ease or Fast fret. Some string makers apply coatings to their strings for the same purpose, and to extend their life.

Talcum powder
Rubbing your hands with talcum powder reduces perspiration. Don't use too much, or else the powder will get into the wound strings and muffle them. Washing your hands with pH-neutral soap may limit perspiration too.

Spare sets
Old strings break more easily than new ones. The more often you change your strings, the less likely it is that they'll give up on you unexpectedly. On the other hand, even a brand new string can break at the first chord. So when you go anywhere with your guitar, always take a spare set with you. Or two, if it's a really important gig.

CHAPTER 8

NEW STRINGS

There are lots of ways to fit new strings. If you do it any of the right ways, your strings will stay in tune as well as they can, and sound good as long as they can. You'll also keep them from damaging your guitar in the process. Here's one of the many right ways to do it, followed by specific tips on replacing nylon strings (page 66) and steel strings (page 69).

Tools Tipcode AGTR-008

Changing strings is easiest with some tools at hand. The first is a *string winder*, which speeds up the job of loosening and winding the strings. The second is a pair of needle-nose pliers to help you get the ends of the strings out of the tuning machines without cutting your fingers. The third is a wire-cutter to remove the excess length of the strings, before or after putting them on the instrument. Some guitarists also use it to cut the old strings, once the tension is off.

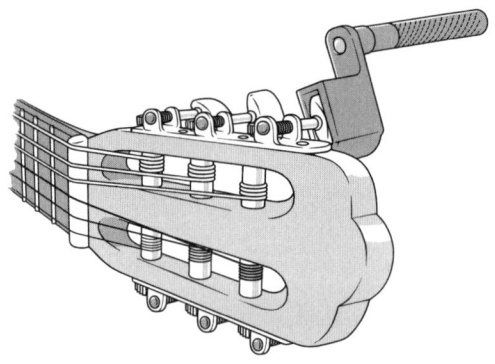

A string winder speeds things up.

The whole set

If one of your wound strings breaks, you may have to fit a whole new set; if you've already been playing the strings for quite a while, a single new one may sound too bright compared to the other wound strings.

Just one

If a plain string breaks, you can usually replace just that one string. Plain strings maintain their sound much longer, so a new one won't usually stand out. That's a good thing, as plain strings tend to break a lot sooner.

One by one

When putting on a new set, it's best to replace the strings one by one. If you remove all the strings before putting on new ones it'll take your guitar some time to readjust to their tension, which may require a lot of extra tuning.

Tuning to the rest

When adding a new set of strings, most guitarists start with one of the two E-strings and replace the next adjacent one, in ascending or descending order. An advantage of this method is that you can tune each new string to the one next to it – assuming that the guitar is in tune to start with. If not, you'll need a tuning fork or something else to give you a reference pitch, or an electronic tuner (see next chapter).

Elasticity

Strings that lose their elasticity lose their sound too. On the other hand, when they're brand new, strings are way too elastic. Put on a new set and you'll find you have to tune them again and again. Most strings don't sound their best until this initial elasticity has been taken away – which is when they start keeping their tuning better as well. With steel strings this only takes a couple of hours. Most types of nylon strings, and especially the plain ones, can easily take one or two days.

Pre-stretching Tipcode AGTR-009

Stretching can be sped up, of course. Slide a finger along the bottom of the strings one by one, and carefully pull them upwards. Retune them. Repeat. And so on, until the tuning is stable.

Cleaning

Some players like to remove all the strings as this allows them to give the fingerboard a good rubdown. There's an alternative way, though, which doesn't require you to take all the strings off at once. First you remove one of the E-strings, creating enough room to take care of that part of the fingerboard. Do the body as well. Then fit the new E-string. Replacing the next strings two by two will allow you to clean the fingerboard between the other strings. Finish with the other E-string.

On the table

When changing strings it's easiest to lay your guitar flat on a table. A big towel or a piece of foam plastic underneath prevents scratches and keeps it from sliding away. Alternatively, you can put your guitar on your lap.

NYLON STRINGS

Putting new strings on isn't really that difficult – especially once you've done it a couple of times.

Removing old strings   Tipcode AGTR-010

Start by loosening the first string, until all the tension is off. A string winder will save you a lot of time. When the string is completely slack, it's easy to remove it. Push it back a little at the bridge to give yourself room to undo the knot. Then pull the string out of the bridge, toward the neck – this way, you don't have to pull the entire string through the bridge.

Cutting the string

Some players cut the slackened string in two places; close to the bridge, and just behind the nut, near the tuning machines. The short leftover pieces are easier and safer to remove than an entire string.

At the bridge...   Tipcode AGTR-011

Once the old string is off, the new string can be tied to the bridge. The first step is shown for the first string (high E), the second for the second string, and so on. This procedure may take some practice at first.

1. Feed the string over the saddle through the appropriate hole in the bridge, until about two inches stick out.
2. Feed this end over the bridge and let it pass under the string.
3. Thread it through the loop. For wound strings just once will do; many players feed the plain strings through the loop three or four times (see the picture).
4. The last 'knot' should always be behind the bridge, not on top of it.
5. Pull the string to tighten the knot.
6. Once the string is tuned, this is how it should look at the bridge.

CLEANING AND CHANGING STRINGS

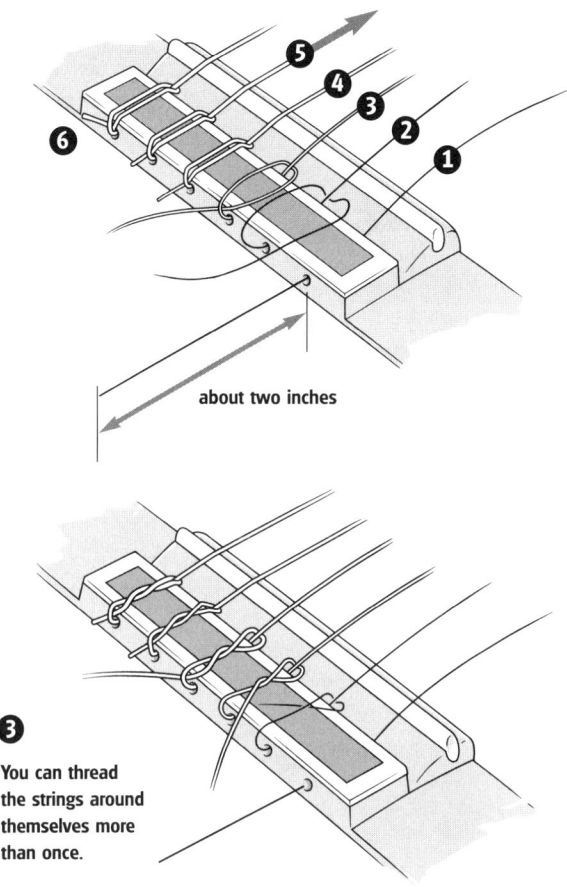

about two inches

3
You can thread the strings around themselves more than once.

... and at the tuner
Tipcode AGTR-012

Similar knots should be made at the other end, at the posts of the tuning machines (see next page). To prevent slipping, the plain strings should be wound around their posts three or four times. For wound strings, three times will do.

1. Feed the string through its post. Leave some slack to allow for the required number of windings.
2. Make a loop, as shown in picture 2.
3. Tighten the string, in the direction of the arrow – the knot should start to look as shown in picture 3.
4. Once the string has been tuned, the knot will look like the one in picture 4.

CHAPTER 8

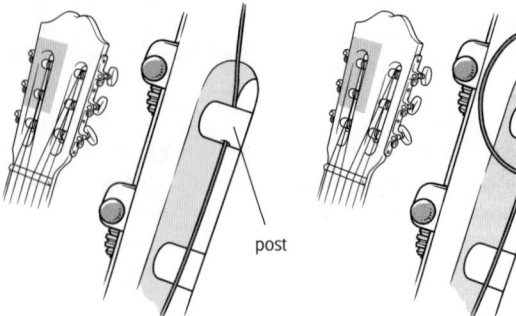

1. Through the hole...

2. Make a loop...

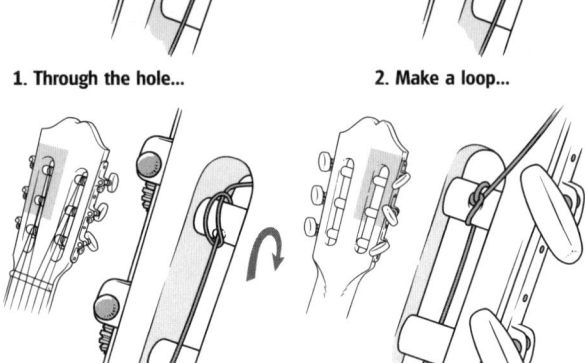

3. The correct winding direction for the post.

4. The resulting knot.

A little tight

To prevent the string from slipping out of its knot at the bridge, you should keep it under a little tension at all times. When winding the string, pull it away from the fingerboard with your other hand, using your index finger to feed it through its groove in the nut. This makes for even windings. The lower illustration on page 72 shows you how.

Inwards and outwards

Both E-strings usually move outwards when winding them, while the other strings will run in the opposite direction, toward the middle of the head.

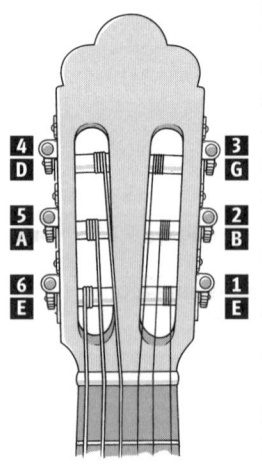

The windings of both E-strings usually run inwards, the others tend to go outwards.

Too long

Most strings are too long. If you attach them to the posts by their ends, you will get so many windings that they get stuck against the inside of the slot. The solution is to leave just enough slack in the string to make the required number of windings. Four to five inches will do, although this is probably a little on the long side – you can cut off what's left once you're done tuning. Once you are more experienced, you can cut the strings to the desired length before putting them on, so that the excess length doesn't get in your way.

Nylon string tips

- Loose ends at the bridge may buzz against the top. Cut them off.
- Instead of pulling the string through the loop at the bridge a couple of times, some players make a knot at the very end of the string. Thread the end with the knot through the loop just once, and make sure it ends up at the back of the bridge. Pull the string tight, and it's fixed.
- Some nylon strings come with ball ends. They have a little ball at the end that replaces the knot; just pull the string through the bridge, starting at the back. Most classical guitarists prefer the traditional knot, though.

STEEL STRINGS

Most steel-string guitars use pins to attach the strings to the bridge. Others come with slotted bridges, similar to the ones on nylon-string guitars. Again, strings need to be completely unwound before removing them. Cutting a

Most steel-string guitars use pins to attach the strings to the bridge.

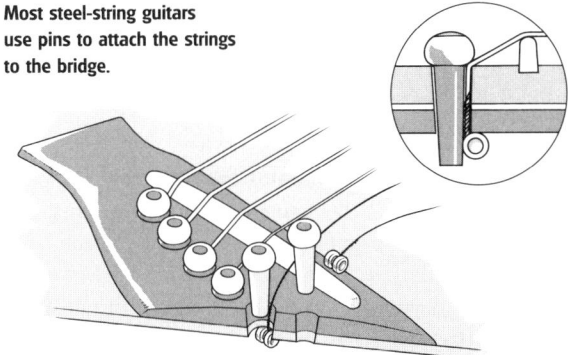

string that is still under tension can easily cause damage to yourself or your guitar.

Cut and remove Tipcode AGTR-013

Unwind the first string, and take it off the tuner post. At the other end, the string is usually attached with a bridge pin. Some string winders have a special notch to remove these pins, and you can also buy a dedicated bridge pin puller. As an alternative you could use a small spoon to lever the pin out of its hole. Other tools can easily damage your guitar. When the pin is out, you can remove the string.

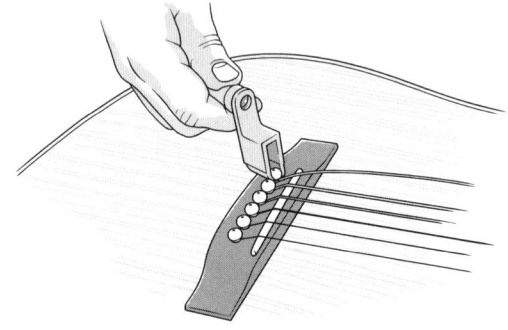

You can easily remove the bridge pins with a string winder.

Attaching the string at the bridge Tipcode AGTR-014

Now make a slight kink near the ball end of the new string, at the point where it will come out of its hole, once fitted. Then insert the ball end into the hole. Let the string run through the groove in the hole, if there is one. Most bridge pins have grooves too; make sure to insert the pin so that the string runs through it. When inserting the pin, lightly pull the string over the bridge, and keep pulling it as you push the pin down. That's it.

Slotted bridge

If the guitar has a slotted bridge, just pull each string through its appropriate hole. The ball ends will secure them. Many roundbacks come with slotted bridges, but you may also find them on other types of guitars. A tip: Go easy when pulling the strings through the bridge in order not to wear them down or cause damage to the guitar or yourself. Strings have sharp ends.

CLEANING AND CHANGING STRINGS

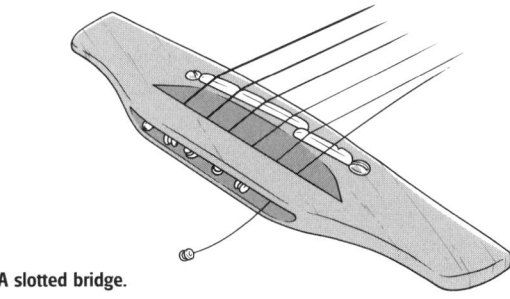

A slotted bridge.

Too long

Like nylon strings, the wound strings should wind around their posts about three times, and the plain ones about four times, to avoid slipping. And just like nylon strings, most steel strings are too long, so don't attach them to the posts by their ends, or you'll end up with too many windings. You can cut them either after they've been fitted or beforehand, leaving about two inches (5 cm) for the windings.

At the tuner   Tipcode AGTR-015

Now attach the string to the post of the tuner. First turn the appropriate post so that the hole is facing the string.
1. Feed the string through the post. Once is enough.
2. Move it over and around the post once.
3. Start winding the string, making sure it now runs underneath the hole.
4. Lift the string from the fingerboard with your other hand, keeping it under a little tension. Use your index finger to guide it through the groove in the nut.

A better tone

String posts have an hourglass shape, with the narrow waist pushing the windings of each string together. If a string is the right length, the windings will be packed together around the waist of the post only. That'll improve the sound and speed up tuning, and your strings will detune less quickly.

String tips

- Make sure you **don't get any kinks in your strings**; kinks can easily cause breakage. There are two exceptions to this rule. One is described on the previous page; the second is that some players use a pair of needle-nose pliers to

make a small kink at the end of each string, so that it hooks around the post.
- You can use the same pair of pliers to **bend the sharp ends** of the strings by the tuning machines down toward the headstock, so you don't prick your fingers.
- It may be hard to tell a thin E-string from a B once all the new strings are out of their bags – so **don't unpack** a string until you're ready to put it on.

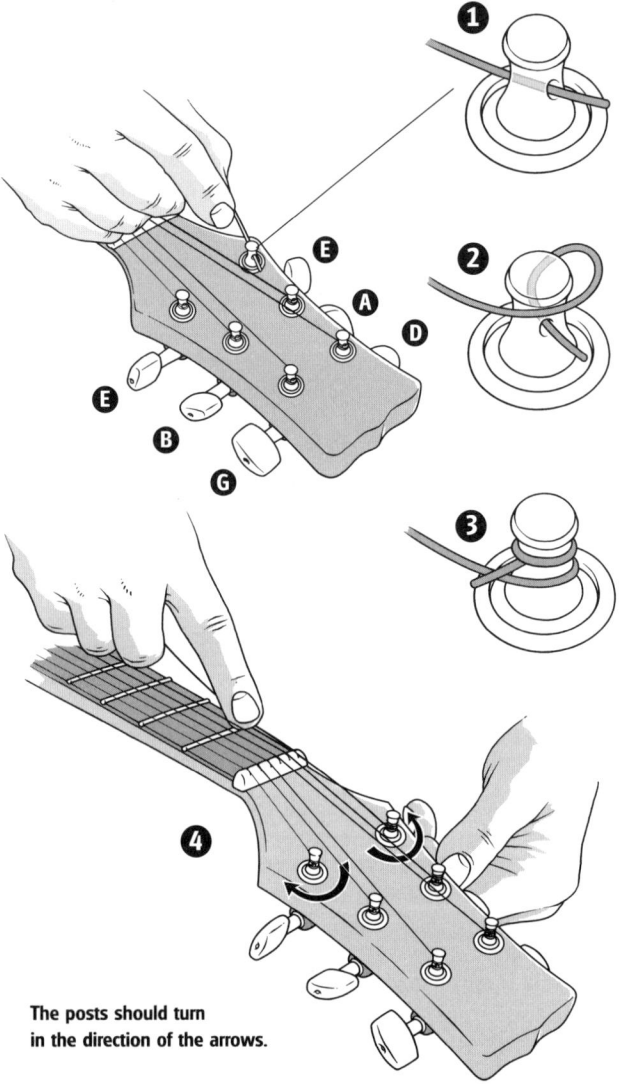

The posts should turn in the direction of the arrows.

- Some manufacturers **print the names** or the numbers of the strings on the bags they're packed in. Others only print the gauges, usually in inches as well as in millimeters.
- Make sure you **never tune your guitar too high or too low**. Strings tend to break and you could damage your guitar if it's tuned too high, while low tunings cause rattles. Besides, a guitar sounds best when it's tuned to its proper pitch, as you'll see in the next chapter.

9. TUNING

Before playing, you have to tune your guitar. Tuning isn't as hard as it may seem at first. You just have to learn how to listen, and you have to know what to listen for and what you're doing. Obviously, you can't learn how to listen just by reading about it – but you'll find everything else in this chapter.

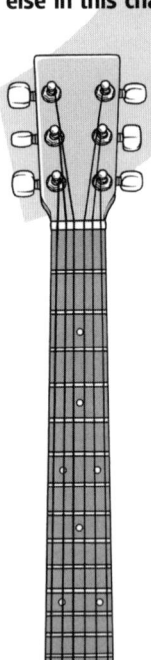

EADGBE

The six guitar strings are tuned to the following pitches:

String	⑥	**E** (the thickest, lowest string)
String	⑤	**A**
String	④	**D**
String	③	**G**
String	②	**B**
String	①	**E** (the thinnest, highest string)

Memory aids

There are many memory aids for these pitches. Three examples:
- Even Adam Did Grow Bored Eventually
- Eating And Drinking Give Brain Energy
- Even After Death Gamblers Bet Everything.

Too low, too high

A guitar sounds at its best when the strings are tuned exactly to these pitches. If the overall tuning is too low, your guitar may still sound in tune, but the strings will rattle against the frets. If the overall tuning is too high the guitar will be harder to play, you'll run a bigger risk of breaking strings, and you may even bend the neck.

Reference pitch

The standard reference pitch to which most instruments are tuned is A4. This is the note that you will hear if you play the high E-string of a well-tuned guitar at the fifth fret. At this pitch, the string vibrates 440 times per second; it's A=440 hertz, in official terminology.

By ear

The easiest way to tune your guitar is to use an electronic tuner (page 81). It's also good to learn how to do it by ear, though, so that's where this chapter starts. For this purpose, you need to start with a reference pitch – preferably A4, as mentioned above.

Piano

A well-tuned piano, or any other keyboard instrument, produces this pitch when you play the A a little to the right of the middle of the keyboard (see page 80).

Tuning fork   *Tipcode AGTR 016* and *AGTR-017*

The same note will sound if you use a tuning fork in A. Just tap this small, thick fork against your knee, say, then – gently – set it against the body of your guitar, or against your ear. That same A can be played back on many electronic metronomes; you can also find it at www.tipbook.com (**Tipcode AGTR-017**).

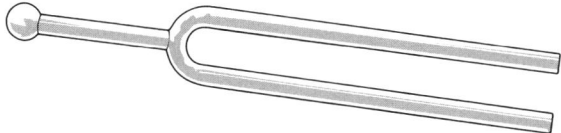

A tuning fork: reliable and affordable.

To the A

First make sure you have A4 as your reference pitch.
- Play the first string (high E), fretting it at the fifth fret. This is supposed to sound an A. Compare it to your reference A.

CHAPTER 9

- If the guitar sounds lower, then carefully tighten the string a bit.
- If it sounds higher, then loosen it carefully.

Two tricks

When you've just started out, it may be hard to hear whether a string sounds too high (*sharp*) or too low (*flat*). Two tricks:

- If a string sounds too high, first loosen it until it sounds obviously too low. Then go up from there. This makes it easier to hear what you're doing, and strings keep their tuning better this way.
- Sing the pitches you hear; you'll easily learn how to 'sense' which one is higher than the other.

The other strings

Once the high E-string is in tune, you can tune the others to it. Basically all you are doing is continuously comparing one string to the other, as shown in the illustration. Fret one string, and compare it to the next one. Here's how.

- Tune the string you're fretting (on the solid dot) to the open string (indicated by an open dot, underneath the string).
- The numbers of the strings are shown at the bottom.
- The names of the strings are shown at the top.
- The letters at the very top show you the two notes you hear when you're comparing strings.

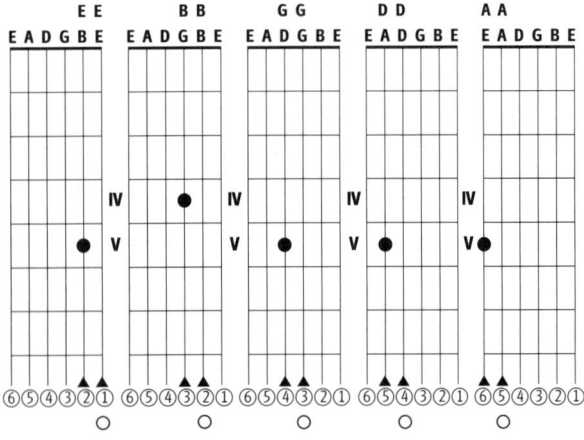

Figure 1. This is how you tune a guitar.

The B, the E, and the rest

Play the B-string at the fifth fret. Compare it to the high E-string you've just tuned.

- Does the B-string sound too low? If so, carefully tighten it.
- Does it sound too high? First loosen it, till it sounds too low. From there, slowly go up again. Then tune the third string to the second, and so on.

The fifth and fourth frets

Most strings are tuned by playing them at the fifth fret, indicated by the Roman numeral V (five). The exception is tuning the third string (G) to the second (B), when you play fret IV.

The other way around   Tipcode AGTR 018

Most guitarists start tuning at the low E, comparing the strings as in the illustration on page 76, but going from right to left. Being the heaviest string, low E doesn't detune that easily, which also makes it a good starting point if you don't have a reference pitch at hand.

Open strings

A major advantage of tuning from low E is that it allows you to tune open strings while fretting the string you've just tuned. This is easier than tuning fretted strings. After all, a fretted string stops sounding as soon as you release it to change its tension. When tuning open strings, you can adjust the pitch while they're still sounding.

Start at the A-string

You can also start tuning at the A-string. One advantage is that you'll hear an A without having to fret a string, which leaves you one hand to hit a tuning fork or piano key. A tip: The open A of this string sounds two octaves lower than the A of a tuning fork, which may make it difficult to compare.

Here's how

First tune the A-string. Now play the A at the fifth fret and tune open D to it. Then tune the other strings, moving from D toward high E. Once high E is tuned, tune low E to it. Double-check low E by playing the fifth fret and compare that pitch to open A.

Slightly higher or lower
Some orchestras or bands may use a slightly higher or lower tuning, for instance A=442; the higher pitch makes for a slightly brighter overall sound. Many electronic tuners can be adapted to other tunings, and tuning forks are available in various pitches.

Tuning fork in E
For guitarists, there are tuning forks that sound the same high E as the first string (E4). One advantage of learning to tune to an A, however, is that this is the pitch most bands, orchestras, and other groups tune to.

HARMONICS
Using harmonics (see page 35) may improve and speed up your tuning. When tuning you will be using the harmonics at the fifth and seventh frets. To really hear them well, touch the string very lightly at the appropriate point with a left-hand finger and strike it firmly, close to the bridge. Playing these harmonics is a bit harder than the ones at the twelfth fret, but you'll be able to do it with a little practice.

Free hand
Tuning with harmonics has a few advantages. First, the strings keep on sounding once you've released your left hand, so you'll have that one free for tuning. Second, it's easier to hear when you've reached the right pitch. How? When the pitches of the two strings are almost the same, you'll hear a wavy sound when you play them together. Now carefully adjust the string you're tuning. The closer you get, the slower the waves will become. At the exact moment the waves disappear, the two strings are in tune with one another; they sound like one. If the waves get faster again, you've gone too far.

Five and seven   Tipcode AGTR-019
Figure 2 shows which strings to compare and which harmonics to play, the latter indicated by solid dots. Instead of the open B-string (which is compared to the harmonic at the seventh fret of the low E-string), you can also use the harmonic at the twelfth fret; this will raise the pitch by one octave.

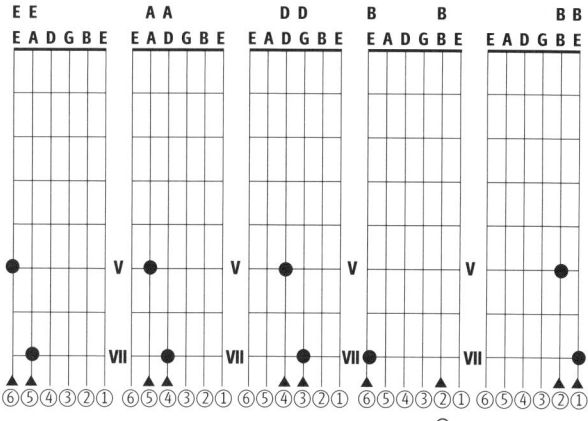

Figure 2. This is how a guitar is tuned with harmonics.

The A

Playing the harmonic at the fifth fret of the A-string produces A4 (A=440).

Twelve-string guitars

Next to each of the four lowest-sounding strings of a twelve-string guitar is a thinner string that sounds exactly one octave higher. The thinner of the two Gs is the highest-sounding guitar string. Both the B and high E-string are accompanied by a second string at the same pitch.

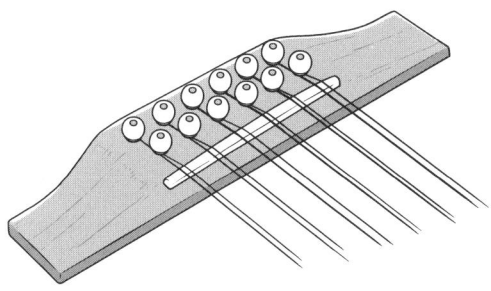

The bridge of a twelve-string guitar.

Acoustic bass guitars

The tuning of an acoustic bass guitar is similar to that of the four lowest-sounding strings on a regular guitar – but they're one octave lower.

CHAPTER 9

Guitar tuning tips
Tipcode AGTR-020

- Of course you can also tune all your strings to the appropriate pitches of **a piano or another keyboard instrument.** You can also find these pitches at www.tipbook.com.

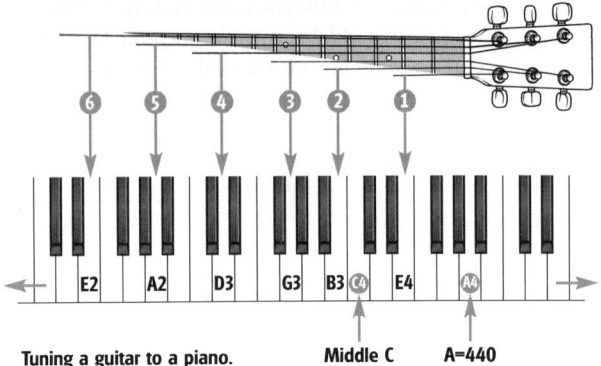

Tuning a guitar to a piano.   Middle C   A=440

- A set of **pitch pipes** can be used too. They're cheap and portable, but they tend to go out of tune rather quickly.
- **Strings detune faster** when they're brand new (be patient, or pre-stretch them: see page 65) or when they slip (put them on right; see pages 62–73).
- If the **nut's grooves** aren't wide enough for the string gauges you're using, tuning may be difficult. A temporary solution is to repeatedly press the string right behind the nut while tuning it. Tune, press, listen, tune... A better solution is to have the nut replaced or adjusted.
- Tuning can be made even smoother if you sprinkle some **graphite** (available at your hardware store) in the grooves, or rub a pencil's point in them.

INTERVALS

Some players prefer to tune their strings by listening to the pitch differences (*intervals*) between the strings, without fretting them or playing harmonics. The interval between the A-string and low E is called a *perfect fourth*.

Amazing Grace

A perfect fourth is what you hear when you sing the first two syllables of *Amazing Grace, Auld Lang Syne, Here Comes the Bride* or *Oh, Christmas Tree*. Sing the first syllable at the pitch that low E gives you; then tune the A-string to the pitch of the second syllable. The same interval is used when going from strings A to D, D to G, and B to high E.

Oh when the Saints
The only interval that's different is the one from G to B; tune it to the first two syllables of *Oh When the Saints Go Marching in*. The name for this interval is a *major third*.

ELECTRONIC TUNERS

Yet another way to tune your guitar is to use an electronic tuner. This is a small device that shows you whether a string is in tune, too high, or too low. On some models you have to set a dial indicating the string you're about to tune. So-called *chromatic tuners* work faster: They simply 'hear' the note you're playing and indicate the pitch it's closest to on the display. A pointer or a series of LEDs will tell you whether you have to tune up or down to get the exact pitch. If you want to use alternative tunings, you'll have to get a chromatic tuner.

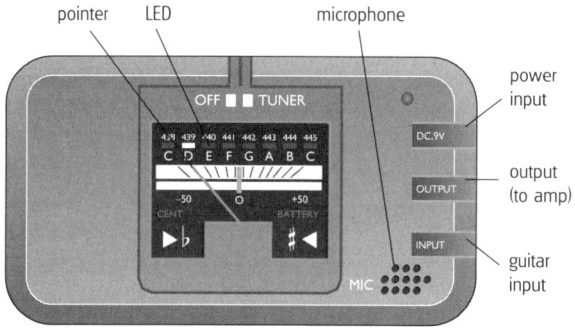

A chromatic electronic tuner indicates which note it 'hears'.

Tips
- **Check your tuning** after you've tuned to an electronic tuner, using any of the methods mentioned above – or all of them.
- If a sharp (♯) lights up on a **chromatic tuner**, the string is sounding a half-tone higher than the tuner indicates, *i.e.*, you're playing an A-sharp (A♯) rather than an A.
- If you buy a tuner for an acoustic guitar, make sure it has

a **built-in microphone**. Most do.
- Some tuners will **automatically switch off** after some five to ten minutes, saving lots of batteries.
- Electronic tuners come **in various price ranges**. For regular guitar tuning, you don't need to spend more than about twenty-five to fifty dollars.

ALTERNATIVE TUNINGS

There are all kinds of different tunings you can use on your guitar – an open tuning for instance, which involves tuning the strings to a specific chord.
Also, you can raise the entire pitch of the guitar by using a capo, making all the strings sound any number of half-tones (half-steps) higher.

Open tuning

Open tunings are very popular. An example would be to tune your guitar, from low to high, to D, G, D, G, B, and D. Strumming the *open* strings will then sound a G-major chord. If a song consists of this type of chords only, you can play it using no more than your left index finger. Place it over all six strings (this is called a *barre*) and simply slide from chord to chord.

Slide

You can also do this with a *slide*. A slide is a tube, usually made out of metal, which you slip over one of your left-hand fingers and slide over the strings. Country and blues guitarists often use this technique. Originally, *bottle necks* were used for slides, and glass slides are still available.

Fingerpicking

The G-major tuning is often used, both for bottleneck playing and for fingerpicking. Fingerpickers also like D, A, D, G, A, D or a similar tuning with the G tuned down to F-sharp or E.

Personal

Some guitarists use their own personal tunings. The open tuning E, A, C-sharp, E, A, E (A-major), for example, was made famous by Bonnie Raitt. C, G, D, A, E, G and E, A, D, G, C F are two tunings used by Robert Fripp (Brian

Eno, King Crimson).
Tip
If an alternative tuning requires you to tune a string way up or down, you may consider using a different string gauge.

A capo Tipcode AGTR-021

For some songs it may be useful to be able to raise the entire tuning of your guitar by any number of half-tone. A capo does that for you: Simply put it in the position where you need it, close to the fret, as you would your fingers (see page 41). There are different capos for classical guitars and steel-string guitars, as their fingerboards don't have the same shape (see page 38). You can get a wide variety of capos for both types of guitars, from very basic models that use a rubber band to clever designs that can be put on and taken off with one hand, or even rolled up and down the neck.

10. PICKS AND NAILS

Most steel-string guitarists use a pick. Classical guitarists pluck the strings with their fingertips and their nails. Fingerpickers do the same, unless they're using special fingerpicks. Flamenco guitarists mainly use their nails.

You can make any guitar sound more powerful, warmer, brighter, rounder, meaner, or smoother, by striking the strings in different positions – close to the bridge, or close to the neck – or by muffling them slightly with the side of your hand. What you use to strike the strings with has a big influence on the sound too. A hard pick yields a different sound than a fleshy fingertip, for instance.

PICKS

Pretty much every music store offers loads of picks to choose from, in all sorts of shapes, weights, sizes, and colors. Bright-colored picks are easier to find once you've dropped them again. Apart from that, your choice mainly depends on what you play, how you play, and what suits you best.

Heavy and light

Each brand makes picks in different weights. A light one may be as thin as ¹⁄₆₄" (less than 0.5 mm). Regular heavy picks are more than twice as thick, and there are much thicker ones too. Heavier picks make for a heavier, thicker, full-bodied sound, both requiring and providing more precision.

PICKS AND NAILS

... in all sorts of shapes, weights, sizes...

Hard or soft
Of course there are light picks that are quite hard, and heavy ones that feel pretty soft and flexible. Just try out a bunch – they cost next to nothing, with the exception of special products such as handmade wooden or bone picks. Also ask other guitarists what they use. Sweaty fingers? Buy a pick with an anti-skid profile or a piece of cork on it, or buy a celluloid one, as this material is less slippery.

Which pick?
For chord playing, most guitarists use soft picks. They're easy to play and make for an even sound. Solo guitarists often prefer smaller, harder picks. Need something really aggressive? Try a metal pick.

Over your fingers
For fingerpicking there are special picks that you slide over your fingers. Banjo players use them too.

Tips
- Check picks for **rough edges**, as they will make your strings wear down fast. Some fine sandpaper or a nail file is all you need to smoothen them up a little.
- Want to play chords and use a pick but your guitar has no **pickguard**? Have one installed, so you won't scratch the varnish off the body. Don't like the look of a pickguard? Get a clear one; they're almost invisible. Also be sure to get a thin one, in order to maintain the sound of your guitar; a heavy pickguard restricts the top – and thus the sound – of your instrument.

CHAPTER 10

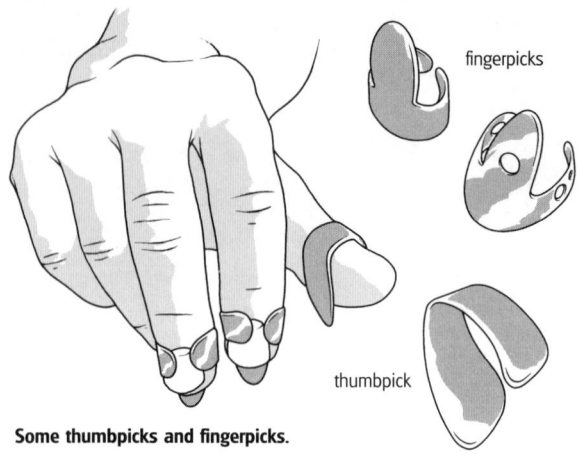

Some thumbpicks and fingerpicks.

NAILS

Flamenco guitarists mainly use their nails to produce their typically fierce sound on a nylon-string guitar. Classical guitarists and fingerpickers may use both their nails and their fingertips. Nails that are too short make for a dull sound, and worn down or split nails don't sound good and may even get caught behind the strings. How do you keep your nails in good shape?

Water and gloves
Water makes your nails go soft. Soapy water is even worse. Try to wear household gloves when you do the dishes or wash your car.

Nail file
For the best results, your nails need to be a certain length and shape. Which length and which shape works best for you depends on more factors than can be dealt with here. Four examples: how hard your nails are, how thick they are, how rounded they are, and how you play… Ask your teacher for advice, experiment, and talk to other guitar players. The same goes for many other nail-related questions.

Textures
To smooth down your nails, you can get files with various textures. Start with a coarse texture, and use the finest for the final step, polishing the tip of each nail to a high gloss.

Good food
A well-balanced diet is important for your nails. White (weak) spots, nails that grow too slowly, or weak nails, to mention a few examples, can all be due to certain food deficiencies. Problems with your nails? Consult a doctor or a dietician.

Nail strengthener
Nails that tear or peel easily may be remedied by using a nail strengthener, available from drugstores. Carefully apply some every couple of weeks until your nails are as hard as you need them to be. From then on just use as much as you need to keep them that way. A warning: If your nails are too hard, they'll break easily – so use strengtheners and similar products in moderation, and keep an eye on your nails.

Personal remedies
Some players combine nail strengthener with nail oil. Others strictly advise against nail strengthener, swearing instead by the use of laurel balm applied daily to cuticles… In other words: There are as many remedies and methods as there are guitarists.

Artificial nails
What if nail strengtheners and other solutions don't do the trick? You could consider artificial nails. Most are not designed for guitar playing, though. Artificial nails used for playing should be strong, and they should very closely follow the shape of your own nails. Some players even make their own artificial nails, in the exact shape they need.

11. MAINTENANCE AND CLEANING

Adjusting and repairing a guitar should be left to a specialized technician. That leaves you to keep your guitar clean and in good working order – both at home and on the road. Here's what you can do yourself, plus some of the things that are best left to a professional.

A crack in the top, a loose brace, a rattle you can hear but can't find, a bridge that comes loose... All good reasons to go see a technician. But there's more.

Action

The action of your guitar will probably need adjusting when you change to heavier or lighter strings: Heavier strings exert more tension, often raising the action, and vice versa. The solution is to either lower or replace the saddle or the nut, or both. Most steel-string guitars have an adjustable truss rod that also affects the action. Adjusting this rod is a job best left to a technician, and it's safest to visit one for any other job that requires tools other than the ones you need to change your strings.

CLEANING

A clean guitar will last longer, it'll be easier to play, and it'll be worth more if you want to trade it in for a better one. Nobody really seems to agree on the best way to clean guitars – there is no 'best way,' obviously. A few tips.

Strings

Cleaning strings has been dealt with in Chapter 8. Please

note that most guitar cleaners should be kept away from strings; what's good for the varnish may be disastrous for your strings.

The fingerboard
When wiping your strings after playing, you can easily clean the fingerboard as well, as described on page 63. If you always do that, you probably won't need to use any of the special fingerboard cleaners that are available. A soft toothbrush may be used to clean the fingerboard where it meets the frets and the nut. Many players treat their fingerboard with a little fingerboard oil or fretboard conditioner, say once a year, to keep it smooth and clean.

Very dirty
Some guitarists use steel wool, liquid, or any other household products to clean dirty fingerboards. These experiments are never risk-free. Steel wool can easily damage more than it cleans, and household detergents may be too abrasive or leave residues. The most important advice? Ask a technician for advice – and bring along your guitar when you do. That way you can also choose to have it cleaned for you…

The body
Cleaning the body is mainly a matter of lightly and frequently wiping it with a dry or slightly moist lint-free cloth. The old T-shirt trick again – but don't use printed ones, as the dye may scratch your finish.

Varnish, varnish, and varnish
Use a dedicated guitar cleaner if you are aiming to seriously clean the body, remove fingerprints and stains, and possibly even restore the finish to its original luster. Please note that special finishes may require special cleaners. What's good for one finish, another can't take. Bodies that are finished with oil or wax also require their 'own' cleaners. Once again, when in doubt, ask your technician for advice, and if necessary bring your guitar along.

Special cleaners
Special guitar cleaners, with names such as *guitar polish*, *guitar juice* or *guitar gloss*, work fine on most instruments.

Some products may be meant to clean only the woodwork, while others are supposed to restore its original luster too. Read the instructions beforehand, then pick one, and read the instructions once more before applying it.

Furniture cleaners
Some guitarists – experienced ones too – happily use the very furniture cleaners that others have warned against for years. A common objection to these cleaners is that they may build up a greasy residue on the instrument's surface. Guitar cleaners are not supposed to do that. Yes, guitar cleaners cost a lot more, but they last a long time too – so you might consider how much you'll actually save by using household products.

Brands
Guitar cleaners are supplied by companies such as D'Andrea, Dunlop, Number One, GHS, and Kyser. Some guitar manufacturers have their own cleaners.

Tuning machines
Open tuning machines can be lubricated with light machine oil. Twice a year will do, using a tiny, tiny drop only. Don't apply the oil directly, but rather dip a match in the oil, then apply it to the tuner. Turn it a couple of times, and you're done. As an alternative you may use some silicone-based slot spray. Again, a tiny bit will do for months. Most sealed tuning machines are self-lubricating.

Dust
A small brush, or a toothbrush as mentioned earlier, will come in handy when removing dust and dirt from the smallest corners. A vacuum cleaner's smallest fitting can be used to remove dust from within the body. Preferably do that when replacing strings; that'll give you more room to get inside.

DRY AIR
When air humidity is high, wood tends to expand. When the air gets too dry, it'll shrink. Sudden humidity changes and low air humidity are among a guitar's worst enemies. If a guitar gets too dry, the braces or the bridge may come

loose, the top may crack, or frets (which don't shrink) may jut out from the sides of the neck (which does). And there's more that may go wrong – so do take care.

Hygrometers
When it comes to air humidity, guitars and people are quite similar: Both like it to be around 50% to 60%. You can check the level of air humidity with a hygrometer, available for some fifteen dollars or more.

Guitar humidifiers
Central heating and air conditioning are two of the main causes of dry air, so take extra care if your house has either, or both. There are all kinds of small affordable humidifiers that can be used inside the case; some are designed to be installed in the soundhole of the instrument. Also, there are cases that have built-in humidifiers, or even a hygrometer and a thermometer.

All-around solutions
If air humidity is very low in your house, both your guitar and yourself may benefit from a central humidifier (if your heating system allows for one) or a portable one. Some examples of the latter are steam humidifiers (affordable, work fast, but may be noisy) and cold humidifier systems which are quieter but more expensive, they take longer to work, and they need frequent maintenance (cleaning, filling, and so on).

Some time to adjust
If you take your guitar some place where the weather is very cold, warm, or wet, always give it some time to adjust to the new surroundings before unpacking it. Take it out after fifteen minutes, or as much longer as you can. The more gradually things change, the better your instrument will like it.

Heaters and windows
Some don'ts: Never store your guitar in direct sunlight, near heaters or fireplaces, or anywhere else where it may get too hot or too cold. If you hang it from a wall at home, preferably choose an inside wall. Sounds a little excessive? According to experts, about ninety percent of all

CHAPTER 11

acoustic guitar problems are related to air humidity or temperature...

Solid tops
Guitars with laminated tops are less sensitive to all of the above than guitars with solid tops – but take care with those as well.

ON THE ROAD

Taking your guitar on the road? Here are a few tips.
- Some twenty-five to fifty dollars buys you a good **gig bag**, but there are cheaper and more expensive versions available too. Most of them have a shock-absorbing inner lining.
- **Compartments or outside pockets** are handy for stashing extra strings, picks, cords, charts, books, or even a music stand.
- Most gig bags come with adjustable, removable **backpack straps**.
- **Check the zipper**. It should be sturdy, and well-covered on the inside, so as not to scratch your instrument.
- Gig bags are less expensive, lighter and easier to carry than **hard-shell cases**, but a good hard-shell case offers better protection against shocks, rain, and other risks. They're more expensive too, generally, ranging from about fifty to four hundred dollars and more.

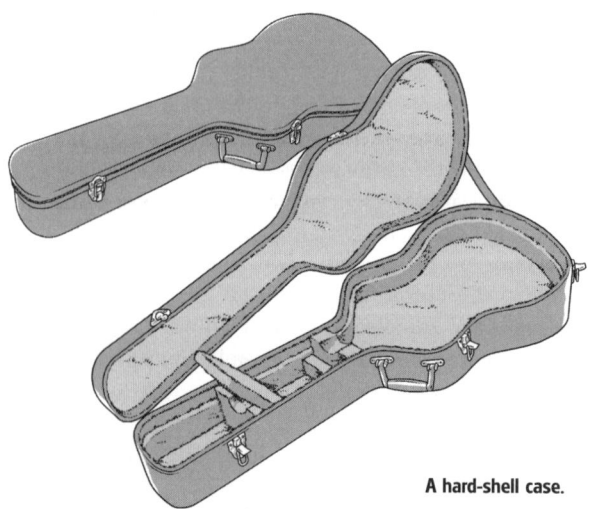

A hard-shell case.

MAINTENANCE AND CLEANING

- Hard-shell cases usually have a molded (plastic) or a plywood core; the term **soft-shell case** usually refers to cheaper models with a core of chipboard, or even cardboard within a thin casing. Incidentally, the same term may also be used to indicate a gig bag.
- **Hard-shell cases** should perfectly fit your guitar. Ill-fitting cases may result in bent necks and other problems.
- Make sure you bring along **spare strings and picks**. If your guitar has a pickup, also take along one or two extra cords, as well as a spare battery (see Chapter 6).
- Taking a break, on the road, at home or anywhere else? Put your guitar in a **special guitar stand**. There's a wide variety of models available, some of them specifically designed to fold up into a very small package, others mainly designed for sturdiness and stability.
- Never leave your stuff in a car **unattended**.
- One of the worst places for a guitar, on the road, is the back shelf of a car, in plain view and direct sunlight. The best place, in a car? **On the back seat**, where it's not as cold (or as hot) as in the trunk.

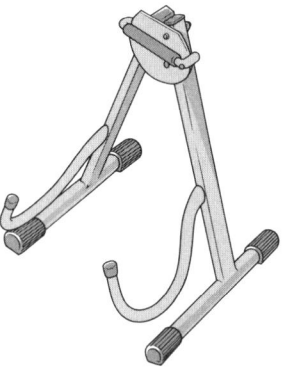

A basic guitar stand.

- Flying out? Then it's best to carry your instrument as **hand luggage**, if that's allowed.
- If your guitar has a **serial number**, you'll probably find it on the back of the head, or on the label or somewhere else inside the body. Jot it down, preferably before your instrument is stolen or lost. There's room to do so on pages 125–126.
- Consider **insuring your instrument**, especially if you're taking it on the road – which includes visiting your teacher. Musical instruments fall under the 'valuables' insurance category. A regular homeowner insurance policy will not cover all possible damage, whether it occurs at home, on the road, in the studio, or onstage.

TIPBOOK ACOUSTIC GUITAR

12. BACK IN TIME

As string instruments have been around for thousands of years, the guitar has many ancestors. There are almost as many stories on how one instrument led to another – and they're often contradictory. In this chapter you'll see some of the main developments; there are plenty of books around that can fill in the details.

Seventeenth century guitar with five pairs of strings.

In the days when supper was still something you hunted, humans discovered that shooting an arrow produces a tone, due to the vibration of the string. Many years later, someone found a way to amplify that sound by attaching a gourd to the bow. And so the first forefather of the guitar was born.

Luthier

Numerous variations on the first string instruments have appeared all around the world, eventually leading to the modern-day guitar. One of its best-known ancestors is the lute (see page 103), which explains why guitar makers are still referred to as luthiers. The first instruments to resemble today's guitar emerged in the sixteenth century. They often had five single or double strings, lacking a low E.

Antonio de Torres Jurado

Some time between 1850 and 1860 the Spaniard Antonio de Torres Jurado built the instrument on which today's classical guitar is based. Torres, as he's usually referred to, combined a slightly bigger body with an improved bracing pattern (fan-bracing) and the current scale – which turned out to be a great recipe. Though his name is still remembered, Torres never really profited from his valuable contributions to the history of the guitar; poverty even forced him to accept other kinds of jobs from time to time... He died in 1892, at the age of 75.

Before nylon

Classical or Spanish guitars have been referred to as 'nylon-string guitars' only for the past fifty years or so, as nylon strings have only been around that long. Before then, gut was used for the plain strings, while the wound strings had a silk core. Nylon strings quickly took over from gut, as they sound brighter and louder, are easier to play as well as more reliable and consistent, and their tuning doesn't drop when air humidity goes up.

THE STEEL-STRING GUITAR

While Torres was working on the classical guitar in Spain, Christian Friedrich Martin was designing the forerunner of today's steel-string guitar in the US.

America

The German luthier Martin (1796–1867) moved to America around the age of thirty-seven. In 1839 he settled in Pennsylvania. About ten years later he developed the X-bracing that is still used for most steel-string guitars.

Not for steel

Contrary to what you may think, Martin didn't come up with X-bracing to deal with the high tension of steel strings; they weren't introduced until the late nineteenth century.

The Dreadnought, first made by the Martin company for a brand by the name of Oliver Ditson, made its debut in 1916. The name Dreadnought (meaning 'fear not') is taken from a large British battleship.

Archtops

In the 1930s, arch-top guitars, which were predominantly used by jazz players, became increasingly popular. The archtop doesn't seem to have had a single inventor, though the name of luthier Orville Gibson, founder of the Gibson company, is often mentioned. The archtop or hollow-body guitar is still favored by most jazz guitarists.

Acoustic/electric

The acoustic/electric guitar gained worldwide acceptance in the early 1980s, Ovation being the first company to equip guitars with built-in piezo pickups on a large scale.

Arch-top guitar with a pickup.

13. THE FAMILY

The acoustic guitar belongs to the huge family of string instruments. In this chapter you'll meet some of its closer family members only, all belonging to the category of fretted instruments – some common, some rare.

As stated in Chapter 5, nylon-string guitars are available in various sizes. Apart from the children's and ladies' sizes mentioned in that chapter, there are quite a few other nylon-string fretted instruments.

Higher and lower
The *requinto*, the main instrument used by Mexican mariachi bands, is just one example of a smaller professional guitar. Another is the *alt* or *alto*, with a scale of about 21¼" (54 cm). Most smaller guitars are tuned higher – a minor third, a fourth, or even a fifth higher, depending on the exact size and use of the guitar. *Baritone guitars* are slightly longer, and they're tuned a bit lower than 'regular' guitars.

Steel-string models
The most popular steel-string models were listed in Chapter 5, from the Dreadnought (a Martin design) to the Jumbo (developed in 1934 by Gibson), the Grand Auditorium, and the Grand Concert. In catalogs you'll often find letters or letter combinations (D, J, GA, GC) used to refer to these models.

Large to small
Rather than using their names, the four medium and

small-sized standard models are sometimes indicated with a code made up of one or more zeros.

- The Grand Auditorium or 'small Jumbo' and similar models have four zeros (0000).
- What some call an Auditorium, others call a Triple-0 (000).
- One size down is the Grand Concert or 00, with dimensions close to those of a classical guitar.
- The single 0 indicates the smallest standard steel-string model, also known as Concert or *porch guitar*.

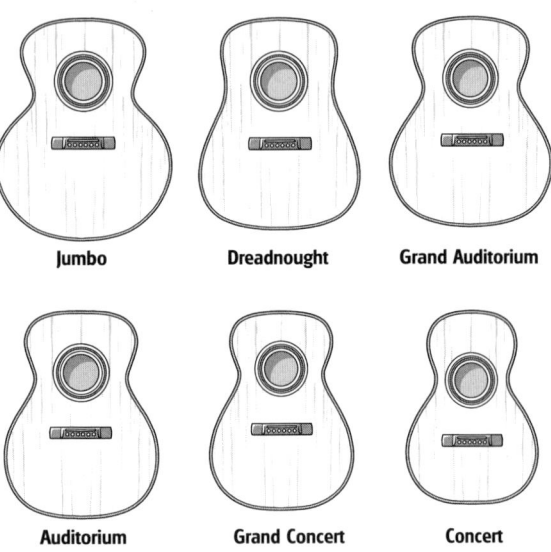

Jumbo   **Dreadnought**   **Grand Auditorium**

Auditorium   **Grand Concert**   **Concert**

More models

The exact dimensions of each model vary from brand to brand, of course, even to the extent that the Grand Concert made by one brand is very close to another brand's Triple-0. Similarly, there are deeper and shallower Dreadnoughts, wider and narrower Jumbos, and so on. Another design is the Orchestra Model (OM), basically a Grand Auditorium with a wider neck and a longer scale. Apart from these standard models, many makers have their own designs.

Small steel-strings

There are also really small steel-string models, which are tuned a bit higher. One example is the *parlor guitar* or *terz* guitar. This short-scale instrument is usually tuned a minor third higher (G, C, F, B-flat, D, G).

More strings

Most guitars have six strings, but you can get more too, the best known example being the twelve-string guitar (page 79). These are usually steel-strung instruments, but there are nylon-string models as well. Guitars with more than six single strings are even rarer, but you may come across instruments with a seventh string, usually tuned to low-A or B, and guitars with ten or eleven single strings.

... and even more?

Electric guitars with two necks aren't that exceptional, but acoustic double-necks are quite rare. The one shown here is a design that has been used by Jimmy Page (Led Zeppelin) and Richie Sambora (Bon Jovi).

Certain styles

Some types of guitars are used mainly in certain styles of music, such as the Selmer and Maccaferri models for flamenco music.

Flamenco

The flamenco guitar is a nylon-string instrument with a body that's often slightly smaller than that of a classical guitar.

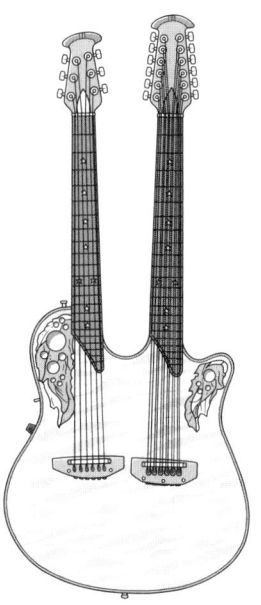

Acoustic/electric double-neck (Ovation).

Combined with a thin top and the use of particular types of wood, this makes for the penetrating, fierce sound of these instruments. Rather than using regular tuning machines, flamenco players often prefer wooden tuning pegs, similar to those of a violin. One or two transparent *golpeadores* protect the top against the nails of the player.

Maccaferri

Around 1930, the Italian guitarist Mario Maccaferri introduced a classical guitar with a cutaway, a large

D-shaped soundhole, and an extra sound chamber, mounted inside the body. The design was rather too revolutionary for classical players, but jazz guitarist Django Reinhardt liked it very much – and to this day you'll find this type of guitar in many gypsy jazz bands. These instruments have steel strings that are attached to a tailpiece, rather than to the bridge. The French Selmer company built Maccaferri guitars for a few years before introducing its own model with a smaller, oval soundhole and no second chamber.

Maccaferri guitar (Van Oosterhout).

Columbus

The requinto or *guitarrico* was one of the instruments that was developed in South and Central America, after Columbus had introduced the guitar to the New World. Some other examples are the five-string *quinto*, the four-string *cuatro* or *quarto*, and the *ukelele* – and there are many more.

Resonator

An eye-catching steel-string variation is the resonator, which usually has a metal body and a top that contains one or more resonators – metal discs that amplify and color the sound. This type of guitar, developed in the US in the 1920s and known for its metallic tone – naturally – is often used by blues musicians, played with finger picks and a

Resonator guitar.

slide. There are basses and acoustic/electric models too. Some call these guitars Dobro's, which is the brand name that was used by the brothers Ed and Rudy Dopyera (Dopyera Brothers). Another well-known brand name is National.

Travel guitars
Some guitars are not designed for a specific sound, but with a particular purpose in mind. Portability, for instance. Two of the many examples of these so-called travel guitars are the Baby Taylor, featuring a short scale and a removable neck, and the Martin Backpacker, available with nylon or steel strings. Other variations include fully collapsible instruments with a metal frame, rather than a traditional body.

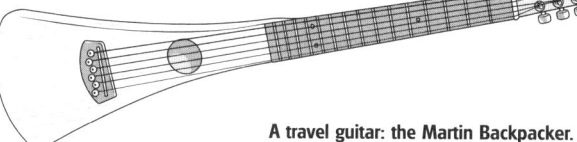

A travel guitar: the Martin Backpacker.

ELECTRIC GUITARS
The main difference between electric and acoustic guitars is that the electric ones need amplification: Instead of a hollow soundbox, which acoustically amplifies the sound, most electric guitars have a *solid body* – and that's what these guitars are known as.

Pickups
Most solid-body guitars have two or three pickups, mounted between the bridge and the neck. A small switch usually allows the choice of any combination of these pickups. The two main types of pickup are single-coils and humbuckers, the latter usually yielding a warmer, rounder, or fatter sound with less hum. Often, the two types are combined on one guitar. If both pickups are the same, the one near the bridge delivers a brighter sound than the one near the neck – comparable to what happens if you play an acoustic guitar near the bridge, or the neck.

Hollowbody
Jazz and blues guitarists usually play arch-top guitars fitted

CHAPTER 13

The two best-known electric guitars: a Stratocaster (Fender) **with three single-coil pickups, and a Les Paul** (Gibson) **with two humbuckers.**

with one or, more commonly, two magnetic pickups. These guitars are often referred to as *hollowbodies*.

More names

Some also call them *full-body guitars*, because they have deep bodies, and others refer to them as *semi-acoustic guitars*. Similar instruments with a shallower body (some two to three inches) are known as *slim-line* or *thin-line guitars*.

Acoustic or electric?

Many guitars are neither fully electric nor completely acoustic. An example would be a 'classic electric' guitar

Electric feel, acoustic sound (Godin).

102

with a shallow, almost solid body (sometimes referred to as a *semi-solid*) and a piezo pickup; or an instrument that plays like an electric guitar yet has a very acoustic sound, or an acoustic/electric with a rather shallow body in the shape of a well-known solidbody… The names of such guitars often indicate what they're about: Classic Electric (Gibson), Acousticaster (Godin), Stratacoustic (Fender), and Ampli-Coustic (Renaissance) are just some examples.

Steel guitar

The steel guitar is yet another variation. It is played horizontally, strings facing up, either on the player's lap (*lap steel*) or mounted on a frame (*pedal steel*), with a slide used to stop the strings. The pedals can be used to change pitch or tunings. Due to its origins, the instrument is also known as the Hawaiian guitar.

MORE FRETTED INSTRUMENTS

There are loads of other fretted instruments, usually with four or more strings. A short introduction, which is by no means complete…

Lute

You don't see too many lutes around today. This ancestor of the guitar has a pear-shaped body, a rounded back, and sides made of wooden strips, a short, wide neck, wooden tuning pegs, and a very intimate, mellow sound.

Mandolin

The original mandolin, with an even shorter neck, is clearly related to the lute. Today most mandolins look quite different, as the illustration shows: They still have a short neck, but they have arched tops (though flat-top models are available too) and, often, a flat back. The four

Mandolin.

pairs of strings are tuned to G, D, A, and E, from high to low. The two G-strings have the same pitch as the G on a guitar. Some variations on the mandolin are the *mandola*, the twelve-string *mandriola*, and the *mandocello*.

Banjo

The *banjo* has a round body and a skin that acts as the top. It has four or five strings and a very short, percussive sound, and is played with finger picks. Five-string banjos, like the mandolin, are mainly used in bluegrass and country, while the four-string is often played in folk and Dixieland bands.

A five-string banjo.

Saz, oud, balalaika...

Many cultures have their own string instruments. Just a few of the hundreds of different variations are the Turkish *saz-baglama*, usually known as the *saz*, with two sets of two and one set of three strings, adjustable frets, a long neck and a relatively small body; the somewhat similar looking Greek four-course (eight strings in four pairs) *bouzouki*; the long-necked Russian *balalaika* with its triangular body; the Bulgarian *tambura* with a very shallow, pear-shaped body, and four double strings… and so on.

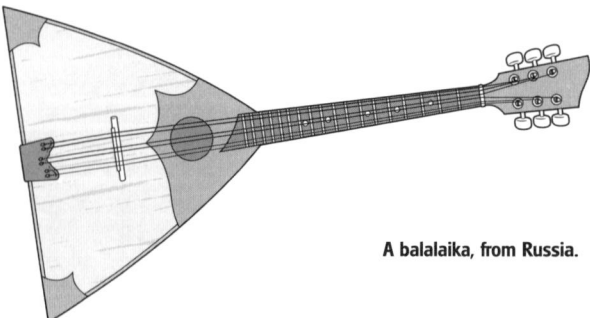

A balalaika, from Russia.

14. HOW THEY'RE MADE

Guitars are made in large plants and small workshops. Though production processes may differ in many ways, the basic principles of guitar construction are quite straightforward.

Tipcode AGTR-022

There are guitar factories where twenty workers produce something like twenty thousand guitars per year. On the other hand, there are luthiers who make one every two months. One major difference? The luthier will carefully hand-pick each and every part, matching them for sound and color – which is unlikely to happen in factory settings.

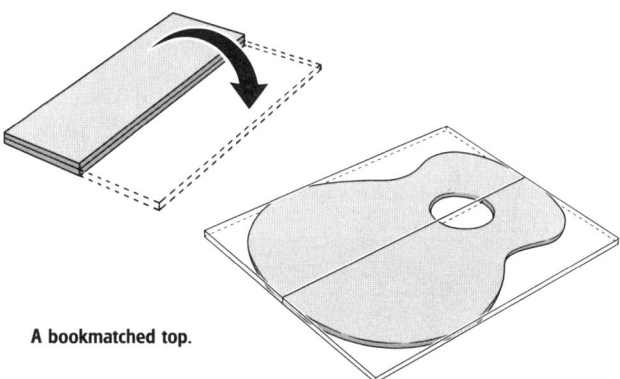

A bookmatched top.

Bookmatched tops and backs

Solid tops are made by splitting a solid piece of wood, resulting in two planks that are the mirror image of each other. Glued together they make a bookmatched top. The same technique is sometimes used for backs, as well as for the outer ply of laminated tops.

The back

The back usually consists of two or three parts. A major difference with the top is that the seams are often finished with a thin strip of wood.

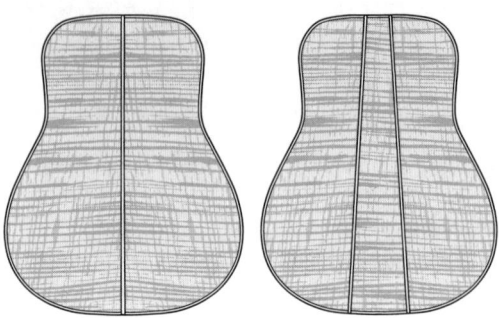

Bookmatched backs, in two or three parts.

The sides

A mold is used to shape the two pieces that make up the sides or rims of the guitar. Alternatively, they may be soaked and then bent, using heat. Thin *linings*, either with or without saw-cuts, provide sturdiness where the sides meet the top and the back. The edges of the body, and sometimes those of the head and the neck as well, are usually finished with wooden or plastic bindings.

Neck, head, and fingerboard

The neck, heel, and head often look like one solid piece of wood, but they're not. Necks are often made of mahogany; this wood is tough and easy to work with, and it doesn't warp easily. The fingerboard is a separate piece of wood that is glued to the neck.

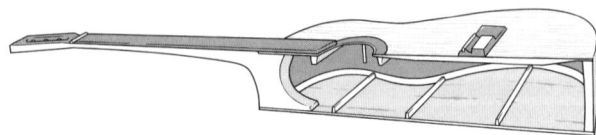

The inside of a classical guitar...

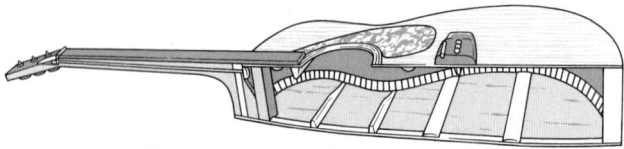

... and the inside of a steel-string guitar.

HOW THEY'RE MADE

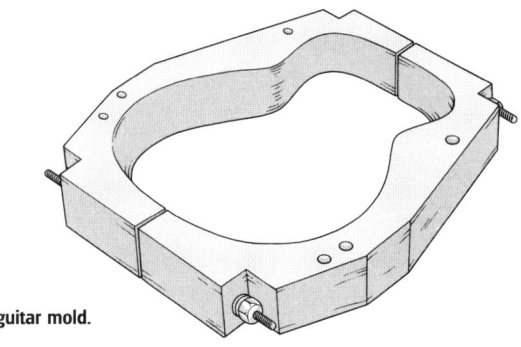

A guitar mold.

Dovetail joint

On most steel-string guitars the neck is attached with a so-called dovetail joint, and a similar construction is used for the necks of classical guitars. Glue keeps everything in place. Some steel-string guitars use screws instead.

Varnishing and finishing

To finish the guitar, a number of thin coats of varnish, up to ten or more, are applied, each one being polished separately. After the hardware has been mounted, the last steps are the fitting of the strings and a final check.

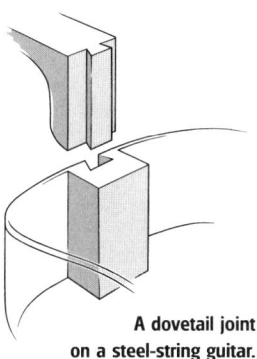

A dovetail joint on a steel-string guitar.

TIPBOOK ACOUSTIC GUITAR

15. BRANDS

Even if we'd severely limited ourselves, a description of each and every guitar brand would easily fill up an entire Tipbook – or two. The following chapter introduces some of the main brands, with an indication of product and price ranges.

There are many more guitar brands than there are guitar factories. Many manufacturers make guitars under various brand names. If your order is big enough, you can have your own brand of guitars made pretty much anywhere on the planet. As a result, you may find identical guitars under different brand names, and they don't always have the same price tag.

Indication
The product line of any guitar brand may suddenly be expanded or discontinued, brand names can disappear or be changed, and distribution may stop or commence, so the following is merely an indication of the brands you may come across, and it's by no means intended to be complete. Please refer to the specialized magazines and websites (see pages 122–123) for up-to-date information.

Nylon and steel
Some brands have both classical and steel-string guitars, as well as electric guitars and bass guitars. Some examples are **Aria**, **Hohner**, and **Samick**, the latter being the trade name of one of the world's biggest guitar manufacturers, supplying instruments for many brands. Other companies make acoustic guitars in pretty much all price ranges, such

as **Takamine**, with its sub-brand **Jasmine**, and **Yamaha**, one of the biggest companies in the music industry, which also makes countless other types of instruments and products.

CLASSICAL GUITARS

Most classical guitars come from Spain, especially from around its capital Madrid, in the middle of the country, and Valencia, a city on the east coast. Many Spanish brands are not available in the US.

Many names

Some Spanish manufacturers concentrate on the low price range only, others make instruments in various price ranges. When shopping for a Spanish guitar, you can come across dozens of brand names, many actually representing the name of the maker. Some examples of well-known Spanish guitar brands, available in various price-ranges, are **Admira**, **Alhambra**, **Amalio Burguet**, **Cordoba**, **Esteve**, **Manuel Rodriguez**, and **Prudencio Saez**. In Spain, guitars are made in small workshops as well as in large factories where traditional craftsmanship and ultra-modern machinery go hand in hand. Some Spanish companies make other guitars as well, including acoustic/electric and steel-string models.

Concert and student guitars

Professional players easily pay two, three, or five thousand dollars – or even more – for a concert guitar. Most of these instruments are made by luthiers who are known only among very limited audiences. Other 'expensive' luthiers grew bigger, employing several makers, and sometimes even offering student models that are made elsewhere. A few examples? José Ramirez IV is a direct descendant of the **José Ramirez** who made his first guitars in 1882. The last hundred-odd years, members of the Ramirez family taught their trade to countless luthiers in the Madrid area. Some other names are **Contreras**, **Conde Hermanos**, and **Bernabe**, the latter having student models made under the name **Antonio Lopez**.

Japan

Contrary to what you may expect, Japan houses quite a

few well-known makers of top-of-the-line 'Spanish' guitars. One example is **Asturias**, with a catalog that includes seven-, ten-, and eleven-string guitars, and a sub-brand (**Kodairo**) representing more affordable models. Concert guitars of more than two thousand dollars are made by **Kohno**. One of the oldest Japanese makers, **Alvarez-Yairi**, makes both classical and steel-string instruments.

Other countries
Of course, classical guitars are being made in many other countries too, often in one-man workshops.

STEEL-STRING GUITARS
The steel-string acoustic guitar is an American invention, and the traditional steel-string guitar brands, like **Martin** and **Gibson**, are still established there. Most of the lower-priced instruments are made in Asian countries, however, and often marketed under 'American' names.

Low, middle, and up
Some brands can be found both in the lower and in the middle price range, sometimes going up to a thousand dollars or more: **Blueridge**, **Cort**, **Crafter**, **Grant**, **Landola**, and **Schecter** for example, or **Epiphone**, **Ibanez**, and **Washburn**. The latter three brands are mainly known for their electric guitars. **Dean** is one of the other companies supplying both acoustic and electric guitars, as well as other fretted instruments. The American **Ovation** company fully concentrates on roundback guitars, with its sub-brand **Applause** for the lower price ranges. **Taylor** is a US maker providing a wide variety of guitars, both in the middle and high-end price ranges.

More US brands
Some other US guitar brands, in a variety of price ranges, are **Doolin**, **Froggy Bottom**, **Grimes**, **H.G. Leach**, **Huss & Dalton**, **Klein**, **McAllister**, **McPherson**, **Tippin**, and **Wechter**. **Alvarez** is probably the best brand to show how complicated the guitar industry really is; its Spanish-sounding name, owned by an American company, adorns Korean-made steel-string guitars that were designed by the Japanese luthier Yairi…

Fender and Gibson

The world's most well-known manufacturers of electric guitars, **Fender** and **Gibson**, also market acoustic guitars. Fender and its sub-brand **Squier** concentrate on the lower price ranges, while Gibson makes higher-priced acoustics only.

Martin

The **Martin** company, founded in 1833, has been very significant for the development of the steel-string guitar. The current president, C. F. Martin IV, is a namesake and direct descendant of the founder. **Sigma** is their lower-priced range of guitars.

Canada

Canada houses quite a few guitar companies. **Larrivee**, **Morgan**, and **Thompson** (the latter two former employees of the first) concentrate on the higher mid-range and above. **Garrison**, a recent addition, features a one-piece bracing system. **Godin** has become especially famous for its semi-solid guitars. **Art & Lutherie**, **Seagull**, **Simon & Patrick**, and **Norman**, are four steel-string guitar brands coming from the same (Godin) company.

And furthermore

Apart from countless little-known one-man workshops, where you can have a guitar completely custom-made by hand, there's a number of small actual brands that concentrate on the high-end market – the Irish companies **Larkin** and **Lowden**, for example, or **Lakewood** and **Stevens** from Germany. In America you have, among many others, **Everett**, **Guild**, **Tacoma**, and **Breedlove**, the latter founded by former Taylor employees. **RainSong**, from Hawaii, uses graphite instead of wood. A few brands where even the least expensive models cost more, to end this section, are **Olson**, **Santa Cruz**, **Dana Bourgeois**, **Goodall**, and **Collings**.

GLOSSARY AND INDEX

This glossary briefly explains all the terminology touched on so far. It also contains some words that haven't been mentioned yet, but which you may come across in other books, in magazines or in catalogs. The numbers refer to the page(s) that contain more information on the subject.

10:1, 12:1, 14:1 *(42)* A set of 10:1 tuning machines offers faster, but less precise tuning than a set of 12:1 or 14:1 tuners.

Abalone *(28)* Mother-of-pearl; product of a shellfish.

Acoustic guitars *(1)* In the old days all guitars were acoustic, and they were just called guitars. It was not until electric guitars came along that traditional guitars had to be specified as being 'acoustic.'
Acoustic instruments can be used without an amplifier – and if you need more volume, you can get yourself a so-called acoustic amp *(53)*.

Acoustic/electric guitar *(14, 48, 49–54)* Acoustic guitar with a pickup and a preamp that can be hooked up directly to an amplifier. Also known as A/E, or as electro-acoustic guitar.

Action *(40–42, 88)* 1. The distance between the strings and the fingerboard, also referred to as string height. 2. The 'feel' or ease of playing of a guitar. A guitar with a great action plays really well and easily.

Adjusting *(41, 88)* A well-adjusted guitar is easier to play.

Amplifier *(53)* Acoustic amplifiers are specifically

designed for acoustic instruments.

Arch-top guitar *(12, 96, 101–102)* A guitar with an arched top and (usually) *f*-shaped soundholes. See also: *Flat-top guitar*.

Auditorium, Grand Auditorium *(29, 98)* Mid-size steel-string guitars; similar models are known as 000 and 0000, respectively.

Back *(33, 105–106)* The back of the body.

Bass guitar, acoustic *(40, 43, 79)* Most acoustic bass guitars have four strings, sounding an octave lower than the four lowest guitar strings.

Bass strings *(9)* The lower sounding (wound) strings of a guitar. See also: *Wound strings*.

Binding *(6, 7, 11)* Ornamental strips that run around the body and sometimes around the neck and the head as well.

Body *(6, 7, 10, 28–30, 105–106)* The body of an acoustic guitar acts as a soundbox, acoustically amplifying the vibrations of the strings. Most electric guitars have solid bodies *(101–102)*.

Bookmatched *(7, 105–106)* A bookmatched top consists of two parts that are each other's mirror image.

Bottleneck *(82)* Used to play slide guitar.

Bracing *(12–13, 34, 95)* A set of braces underneath the top, which influence the sound and reinforce the wood. Most classical guitars have fan-bracing, while X-bracing is still very popular on steel-string guitars. Some of the alternatives are horizontal, A- and V-bracings.

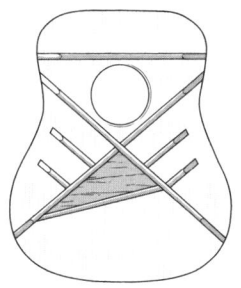

A-bracing.

Bridge *(6, 9, 10, 11)* The strings are attached to the body at the bridge, and run over the saddle or bridge saddle. See also: *Bridge saddle* and *Nut*.

Bridge pins *(10, 11, 69–70)* The pins that secure

the strings of a steel-string guitar to the bridge.

Bridge saddle *(6, 9, 10, 11, 44)* Thin strip, usually plastic, that supports the strings, just before the point where they're attached to the bridge. Many steel-string guitars have a *compensated saddle*, which is slightly adjusted to enable optimal intonation. See: *Intonation*.

Camber See: *Radius*.

Capo *(41, 83)* By mounting a capo (from the Italian 'capo d'astro') on the neck of a guitar, you can raise the overall pitch in half-tones.

Classical guitar *(2–3, 6–9)* Acoustic guitar with nylon strings. Also referred to as Spanish guitar or nylon-string guitar.

Concert, Grand Concert *(29, 98)* Smaller-sized steel-string guitars.

Concert guitar *(23, 109)* Expensive classical guitar for professional performances. However, the same name is used for the low-budget models of low-budget brands too. Conversely, some well-known luthiers make 'student guitars' with thousand-dollar price-tags…

Custom Many luthiers will make guitars exactly according to the customer's specifications. Some expensive brands offer custom options, such as a choice between various necks or tops.

Cutaway *(11, 30–31)* A cutaway allows for easier access to the highest frets.

Dobro See: *Resonator guitar*.

Dreadnought *(28–29, 97–98)* Big-size steel-string guitar.

Ebony *(35)* Hard type of wood, often used for fingerboards.

Electro-acoustic guitar See: *Acoustic/electric guitar*.

Electronic tuner *(81)* Tuning device.

Element See: *Pickup*.

Fan-bracing See: *Bracing*.

Feedback *(50–54)* Amplified acoustic guitars are notorious for producing the loud *skreeee* that's known as feedback. A loudspeaker produces a sound that makes the pickup vibrate, resulting in a signal that is sent to the amp to be reproduced by the same loudspeaker, which again sets the pickup to vibrate, and so on… See also: *Notch filter*.

Fingerboard *(6, 8, 10, 35–40, 89)* Also known as fretboard; the face of the neck, on which you put four of your fingers.

Fingerpicking *(29, 38, 84)* Steel-string guitar playing style; the thumb takes care of the bass part, the other fingers play the melody.

Flageolet See: *Harmonic*.

Flamenco guitar *(33, 41, 99)* Very similar to a classical guitar, but often a bit smaller, with a thin top, a cypress back, one or two pickguards (*golpeador*), and a rather low action.

Flat-top guitar *(12)* Steel-string guitar with a flat top, as opposed to an arched top. Classical guitars have flat tops too, but there's no need to refer to them as such; there are no classical arch-top guitars. See also: *Arch-top guitar*.

Folk guitar See: *Steel-string guitar*.

Fourteen-fret neck *(9, 40)* A neck that joins the body at the fourteenth fret. Most steel-string guitars have fourteen-fret necks. See also: *Twelve-fret neck*.

Fretboard See: *Fingerboard*.

Frets *(6, 8, 10, 43, 48, 62)* The metal strips on the fingerboard or fretboard.

Golpeador *(99)* Spanish for pickguard. See also: *Flamenco guitar*.

Grand Auditorium, Grand Concert *(29, 98)* Steel-string guitar sizes.

Harmonic *(35–36, 78–79)* The tone you hear when striking a string that's not pressed down at a fret, but lightly touched exactly halfway (above the twelfth fret), or at a third, a quarter (et cetera) of the string's length. Also known as *overtone* or *flageolet*.

Head, headstock *(5, 6, 10)* The end of the neck. Classical guitars have slotted heads; most steel-string guitars have a solid head. Another name: *peghead*.

Heel *(6, 8, 10,)* The thick part where the neck joins the body.

Hygrometer *(91)* Device that indicates the degree of air humidity.

Inlay *(23, 27–28)* The markers, the decoration around the soundhole, and also the bindings are often inlaid pieces of wood or other materials. See also: *Abalone*.

Insurance *(93)* Smart.

Intonation *(35–36, 44, 56)* A guitar is supposed to have proper intonation; when playing the twelfth fret all strings should sound exactly one octave higher than when they're being played open.

Jumbo *(28–29, 97–98)* The biggest size of the regular steel-string guitar.

Laminated *(31, 33, 92)* A laminated top, back, or side consists of a number of thin plies of wood. See also: *Solid*.

Left-handed *(13–14)* Classical guitars are quite easy to adapt for lefties, contrary to steel-string guitars – but of course 'left-handed' guitars are available.

Lower bout *(6, 7, 10)* Lower, broader part of the body.

Luthier *(7, 23, 105)* Guitar maker (literally: lute maker).

Machine head One of the many names for tuner or tuning machine.

Markers *(6, 8, 10, 11, 28)* Dots, figures, or blocks which tell you which fret you are at.

Melody strings See: *Plain strings*.

Nails *(86–87)* Important, non-replaceable accessories for classical players, flamenco guitarists, and fingerpickers.

Neck *(6, 7, 10, 11, 35–40, 106)* Joins the body and the head.

Notch filter *(50)* An adjustable filter to prevent feedback. See also: *Feedback*.

Nut *(6, 9, 10, 44, 80)* Small part, often plastic, that separates the head and the neck, keeping the strings at the right distance from each other.

Overtone See: *Harmonic*.

Open tuning *(82)* Alternative guitar tuning.

Peg, peghead See: *Tuner* and *Head*.

Pick *(84–85)* Usually a triangular piece of plastic,

in different weights. Playing with a pick gives a more penetrating sound than playing with your fingers. Another name: plectrum.

Pickguard *(9, 10, 85, 99)* Thin plastic plate that protects the body against scratching picks and nails.

Pickup *(14, 49–52, 96, 101)* A pickup or transducer converts the vibrations of the strings into electrical signals. Acoustic/ electric guitars usually come with piezo-electric pickups that are located under the guitar's bridge saddle. This type of pickup responds to both steel and nylon strings, unlike magnetic pickups. See also: *Acoustic/ electric guitar.*

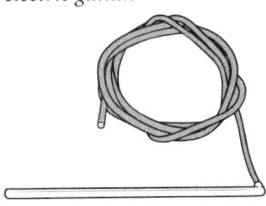

Piezo pickup.

Plectrum See: *Pick.*

Plain strings *(9, 11, 57, 58)* The thin, unwound strings, also called *melody strings* or *trebles.*

Posts, *(6, 10, 55)* The (string) posts that actually wind the strings.

Preamp, preamplifier *(14, 49, 51–52, 54)* Amplifies the weak signal of a built-in pickup before sending it to the main amp or power amplifier. Most acoustic/ electric guitars have built-in preamps.

Price indications *(22–25, 50)* How much do guitars cost?

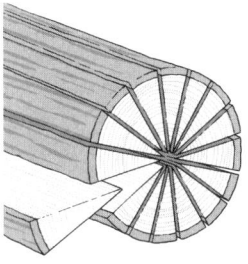

Quarter-sawn wood is stronger that slab-cut wood.

Quarter-sawn When you saw a tree into quarterings, you get stronger wood that allows for the production of thin, yet strong tops. Provides less and therefore more expensive wood than *slab-cutting* or *plain-sawn* trees.

Radius *(38)* The curve of the fingerboard. On steel-string guitars, the fingerboard is a bit rounded; it's higher underneath the middle strings. The degree of this radius or camber is expressed in inches. The higher the number, the flatter the fingerboard.

Resonator guitar *(100–101)* Guitar with amplifying, metal resonators in the top. Also known as Dobro, a trade name.

Rosette *(6, 7, 10, 27–28)* The decoration of the soundhole.

Roundback *(29–30, 70)* Guitar with a round back, usually acoustic/electric.

Saddle See: *Bridge saddle.*

Scale *(39–40, 97)* The vibrating length of the strings, measured from the nut to the saddle.

Semi-acoustic guitar *(102)* A name often used for arch-top guitars with built-in pickups.

Semi-solid guitar *(103)* A guitar with an 'almost but not entirely' solid body.

Sides *(6, 10, 33, 106)* Between the top and the back are the sides. They are always made up of two parts, each one running from the heel to the tail of the body.

Slotted bridge *(70–71)* Classical guitars and some (mainly roundback) steel-string guitars have slotted bridges with the strings running through them. See also: *Roundback.*

Slotted head See: *Head.*

Solid *(22, 31, 32, 92, 105)* A solid top, made out of a split, single piece of wood, enhances the sound of a guitar. Some guitars also have solid backs and sides. See also: *Laminated.*

Soundboard Another word for top. See also: *Top.*

Soundbox See: *Body.*

Soundhole *(6, 7, 10, 34–35)* The size and location of the soundhole also affects the timbre of the instrument.

Spanish guitar *(2–3)* Another name for classical guitar. Just to make it more confusing, a flamenco guitar is a Spanish guitar too, but it's a different instrument. And there are lots of other countries where 'Spanish' guitars are made… See also: *Classical guitar.*

Steel-string guitar *(3, 9–12)* Generic name to indicate a guitar with steel strings and a flat top. Also called western guitar, folk guitar, or flat-top guitar.

Strings *(8–9, 11, 55–61);*

changing strings *(64–73)*.

String posts See: *Posts*.

String winder *(64)* Tool to speed up loosening or tightening strings. Some models help in removing bridge pins too.

Student guitar *(23)* See: *Concert guitar*.

Top *(6, 7, 10, 12, 22, 31–34, 55, 92, 105)* The top of the body; also known as soundboard.

Transducer See: *Pickup*.

Treble strings, trebles See: *Plain strings*.

Triple-0 *(29, 98)* Mid-size steel-string guitar, comparable to an Auditorium. See: *Auditorium, Grand Auditorium*.

Truss rod *(11, 37, 41, 88)* Usually a metal, adjustable rod that reinforces (trusses) the neck of a steel-string guitar.

Tuner, tuning machine *(6, 8, 10, 42, 43, 48)* Each string has its own tuning machine. Classical guitars have open tuners, steel-strings usually have sealed ones. Some other names are *machine head*, *tuning head*, *tuning key*, and *tuning gear*. The wooden tuners on flamenco guitars are called *pegs*, and this word is used for the tuners of other guitars too.

Twelve-fret neck *(40)* Has more than twelve frets, but the twelfth fret is the one where the neck joins the body, as on classical guitars. See also: *Fourteen-fret neck*.

Twelve-string guitar *(79)* Almost always a steel-string guitar, but there are also nylon-string guitars with twelve strings.

Upper bout *(6, 7, 10)* Upper, broader part of the body.

Varnish *(27)* The type and the quality of the varnish

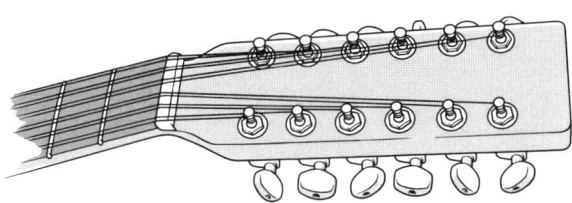

The head of a twelve-string guitar.

may influence the sound, the appearance, and the way a guitar should be cleaned.

Waist *(6, 7, 10)* The narrow part of the body.

Western guitar Another name for steel-string guitars. See: *Steel-string guitar*.

Wound strings *(9, 11, 56–59)* Strings that are wound with thin metal wire.

X-bracing See: *Bracing*.

TIPCODE LIST

The Tipcodes in this book offer easy access to short movies, photo series, soundtracks, and other additional information at www.tipbook.com. For your convenience, the Tipcodes in this Tipbook have been listed below.

Tipcode	Topic	Chapter	Page
AGTR-001	Playing classical guitar	1	1
AGTR-002	Classical & steel-string guitars	2	7
AGTR-003	The blues	3	16
AGTR-004	Playing chords	5	29
AGTR-005	Fingerpicking	5	29
AGTR-006	Checking the intonation	5	35
AGTR-007	Left-hand technique (classical)	5	37
AGTR-008	String winder	8	64
AGTR-009	Pre-stretching strings	8	65
AGTR-010	Removing nylon strings	8	66
AGTR-011	Putting on a nylon string (bridge)	8	66
AGTR-012	Putting on a nylon string (tuner)	8	67
AGTR-013	Removing a bridge pin	8	70
AGTR-014	Putting on a steel string (bridge)	8	70
AGTR-015	Putting on a steel string (tuner)	8	71
AGTR-016	A=440 (reference pitch)	9	75
AGTR-017	Tuning fork	9	75
AGTR-018	Tuning	9	77
AGTR-019	Tuning with harmonics	9	78
AGTR-020	String pitches: E, A, D, G, B, E	9	80
AGTR-021	Using a capo	9	83
AGTR-022	Making a guitar	14	105

WANT TO KNOW MORE?

Tipbooks give you basic information on the instrument of your choice and everything connected with it. Of course, there's a lot more to be found on all the subjects you come across on the previous pages.
A selection of magazines, books, and websites, as well as some background on the makers of the Tipbook series.

MAGAZINES

Some of these magazines concentrate on acoustic guitars, others focus on electric instruments but include acoustics as well, still others concentrate on a certain style of guitar playing.

- *Acoustic Guitar,* www.acguitar.com
- *Fingerstyle Guitar,* www.fingerstyleguitar.com
- *Flatpicking Guitar,* www.flatpick.com
- *Guitar One,* www.guitaronemag.com
- *Guitar Player,* www.guitarplayer.com
- *Guitar Review,* www.guitarreview.com
- *Guitar Techniques,* www.futurenet.com
- *Guitar World Acoustic,* www.guitarworld.com
- *Guitarist,* www.futurenet.com
- *Vintage Guitar Magazine,* www.vintageguitar.com

BOOKS

There are countless books on guitars, including publications dedicated to one guitar brand only. The list below contains a variety of books, some concentrating on the history of the instrument, others more technically oriented, some also including electric guitars and basses, others dedicated to acoustic instruments only. Please note that this list is not intended to be complete.

- *The Ultimate Guitar Book*, Tony Bacon and Paul Day (Knopf, 1997; 192 pages; ISBN 0 375 70090 0).
- *The Guitar Handbook*, Ralph Denyer (Knopf, 1992; 256 pages; ISBN 0 679 74275 1).
- *The Complete Guitarist* (Richard Chapman, DK Publishing, England, 1993; 191 pages; ISBN 075130 018 7).
- *The Acoustic Guitar Guide*, Larry Sandberg (A Capella Books, 2000; ISBN 1 55652 418 8).
- *Acoustic Guitar Owner's Manual – The Complete Guide* (String Letter, Hal Leonard, 2000; 96 pages; ISBN 1 890490 21 0).
- *American Guitars – An Illustrated History*, Tom Wheeler (Harper Collins, 1992; 384 pages; ISBN 0 062 73154 8).
- *Custom Guitars – A Complete Guide to Contemporary Handcrafted Guitars* (String Letter, 2000; 152 pages; ISBN 1 890 49029 6).
- *Gruhn's Guide to Vintage Guitars – An Identification Guide for American Fretted Instruments*, George Gruhn, Walter Carter (Backbeat Books, 1999; 581 pages; ISBN 0 879 30422 7).
- *Acoustic Guitars and Other Fretted Instruments – A Photographic History*, George Gruhn, Walter Carter (Backbeat Books, 1997; 320 pages; ISBN 0 879 30493 6).
- *Blue Book of Acoustic Guitars,* by Steven Cherne and S.P. Fjestad (Blue/Black, 2000; 400 pages; ISBN 1 886 78681 X).
- *Guitars – From the Renaissance to Rock; Music, History, Construction and Players*, by Tom and Mary Anne Evans (Paddington, USA/UK, 1977; 479 pages; ISBN 0 488 22240 X).
- *The Acoustic Guitar*, Nick Freeth and Charles Alexander (Courage Books, USA/UK, 1999; 159 pages; ISBN 07 624 0419 1).

INTERNET

The Internet offers lots of information on guitars. One of the easiest ways to discover what's there is to visit one of the sites below. All of them offer loads of links to other sites (makers, musicians, education, etc.) as well as other services: acoustic-guitars.net, guitarist.com, guitarnotes.com, guitarsite.com, wholenote.com, and worldguitarist.com. More websites can be found in the above list of magazines.

ABOUT THE MAKERS

Journalist, writer, and musician *Hugo Pinksterboer*, author of the Tipbook Series has published hundreds of interviews, articles, and instrument, video, CD, and book reviews for national and international music magazines. He wrote the reference work for cymbals (*The Cymbal Book*) and has written and developed a wide variety of manuals and courses, both for musicians and non-musicians.

Illustrator, designer, and musician *Gijs Bierenbroodspot* has been the art director for a wide variety of magazines, and has developed numerous ad campaigns. While searching for information about saxophone mouthpieces, he got the idea for this series of books on music and musical instruments – and has created the layout and the illustrations for them as well. He has also found a good mouthpiece, by the way.

ESSENTIAL DATA

In the event of your equipment being stolen or lost, or if you decide to sell it, it's useful to have all the relevant data at hand. Here are two pages to make those notes. For the insurance, for the police or just for yourself.

INSURANCE

Company:	
Phone:	Email:
Agent:	
Phone:	Email:
Policy no.:	
Premium:	

INSTRUMENTS AND ACCESSORIES

Make and model:	
Serial number:	
Value:	
Specifications:	
Date of purchase:	Bought at:
Phone:	Email:

Make and model:	
Serial number:	
Value:	
Specifications:	
Date of purchase:	Bought at:
Phone:	Email:

Make and model:	
Serial number:	
Value:	
Specifications:	
Date of purchase:	Bought at:
Phone:	Email:

THE TIPBOOK SERIES

TIPBOOK SERIES
MUSIC AND MUSICAL INSTRUMENTS

AM990462 – **Tipbook Drums**   ISBN 978-1-84772-071-9
AM990473 – **Tipbook Acoustic Guitar**   ISBN 978-1-84772-072-6
AM990484 – **Tipbook Vocals**   ISBN 978-1-84772-073-3
AM990495 – **Tipbook Electric Guitar & Bass**   ISBN 978-1-84772-074-0
AM990506 – **Tipbook Saxophone**   ISBN 978-1-84772-075-7
AM990517 – **Tipbook Basic Music Theory**   ISBN 978-1-84772-076-4

Take a look at www.musicsales.com.